The Septuagint and the Greek New Testament

Bridging Ancient Scriptures with Early Christian Writings

Christian Norris

Copyright © 2024 by CHRISTIAN NORRIS
All rights reserved. No part of this publication may be reproduced, stored or transmitted in any form or by any means, electronic, mechanical, photocopying, recording, scanning, or otherwise without written permission from the publisher. It is illegal to copy this book, post it to a website, or distribute it by any other means without permission.

Table of Contents

Introduction   **5**
Chapter 1   **11**
Origins of the Septuagint   11
Historical Background   11
Translation Process   15
Chapter 2   **21**
The Canon and Text of the Septuagint   21
Books Included   21
Variations and Manuscripts   25
Chapter 3   **29**
The Influence of the Septuagint in Hellenistic Judaism   29
Jewish Diaspora and the Septuagint   29
Use in Jewish Worship   34
Chapter 4   **41**
The Septuagint in Early Christianity   41
Quotations in the New Testament   41
Theological Implications   48
Chapter 5   **55**
The Greek New Testament: Formation and Canon   **55**
Writing and Compilation   55
Canonical Criteria   61
Chapter 6   **69**
Comparative Analysis of the Septuagint and the Greek New Testament   69
Linguistic and Stylistic Features   69
Shared Themes and Concepts   75
Chapter 7   **83**

The Role of the Septuagint in the Early Church	**83**
Patristic Writings and Exegesis	83
Liturgical Use	89
Chapter 8	**95**
Textual Criticism and the Septuagint	95
Methods and Challenges	95
Major Critical Editions	100
Chapter 9	**107**
Modern Translations and the Septuagint	107
Influence on Contemporary Bibles	107
Translational Philosophies	113
Chapter 10	**119**
Theological Reflections on the Septuagint and New Testament	119
Christological Interpretations	119
Old Testament Prophecies and Fulfillment	125
Conclusion	**131**

Introduction

The Septuagint, an ancient Greek translation of the Hebrew Bible, holds profound significance not only for the Jewish Diaspora of antiquity but also for the early Christian church. This book aims to elucidate the intricate relationship between the Septuagint and the Greek New Testament, providing a comprehensive understanding of how these texts shaped theological thought and biblical interpretation. By examining the historical, linguistic, and theological dimensions of these scriptures, we gain insights into their enduring influence on religious traditions and scholarly pursuits.

This book bridges the gap between ancient scriptures and early Christian writings, offering readers a detailed exploration of the Septuagint and the Greek New Testament. By delving into the origins, canon, textual variations, and theological implications of these texts, we seek to uncover the profound connections that have shaped the foundations of Judeo-Christian beliefs. This work is intended for scholars, theologians, and lay readers who seek to deepen their understanding of the Bible's historical context and its enduring spiritual significance.

Studying the Septuagint and the Greek New Testament together is essential for several reasons. Firstly, the Septuagint was the primary scripture for many early Christians, including the authors of the New Testament.

It provided a linguistic and conceptual framework that influenced their writings and theological formulations. For instance, when the New Testament writers quoted the Old Testament, they often did so from the Septuagint rather than the Hebrew text. This preference highlights the Septuagint's role in shaping early Christian thought and its perceived authority among the early believers.

The Septuagint's translation of Hebrew scriptures into Greek made these texts accessible to a broader audience within the Hellenistic world. This accessibility was crucial for the spread of Judaism and Christianity among Greek-speaking populations. The use of a common language facilitated the transmission of religious ideas and the integration of diverse cultural elements. As a result, the Septuagint became a bridge between Jewish and Greco-Roman cultures, allowing for a richer exchange of theological and philosophical concepts.

The Septuagint's linguistic choices and interpretative renderings often differ from the Hebrew text, offering unique theological insights. These differences can shed light on how ancient Jewish communities understood their scriptures and how these interpretations influenced early Christian theology. For example, certain messianic prophecies in the Septuagint are more explicitly linked to Jesus Christ in the New Testament, suggesting that early Christians saw these translations as prophetic validations of their beliefs.

The comparative study of the Septuagint and the Greek New Testament also enhances our understanding of the development of biblical canon and textual criticism. The process of canon formation in early Christianity was influenced by the texts available to early believers, and the Septuagint played a pivotal role in this process. By examining the criteria and debates surrounding the inclusion of books in the biblical canon, we gain insights into the historical and theological contexts that shaped the Bible as we know it today.

Textual criticism, the scholarly discipline of evaluating and comparing manuscripts to determine the most accurate text, is another area where the Septuagint and the Greek New Testament intersect. The variations and manuscript traditions of the Septuagint provide critical data for understanding the transmission and preservation of biblical texts. This analysis not only helps in reconstructing the original texts but also reveals the historical and cultural factors that influenced their transmission.

In addition to these scholarly pursuits, studying the Septuagint and the Greek New Testament together has significant theological implications. The Septuagint's translation choices can affect the interpretation of key biblical themes, such as covenant, salvation, and prophecy. By comparing these themes across both bodies of scripture, we can trace the development of theological concepts and their impact on Christian doctrine. For instance, the concept of the New

Covenant, central to Christian theology, is rooted in the Septuagint's interpretation of Old Testament promises and their fulfillment in the New Testament.

Furthermore, the early church's use of the Septuagint in liturgy, catechesis, and exegesis underscores its importance in shaping Christian worship and doctrine. Church Fathers such as Augustine, Origen, and Jerome engaged deeply with the Septuagint, using it to explain and defend Christian teachings. Their writings provide valuable insights into how the Septuagint was understood and utilized in the early church, highlighting its role in the development of Christian thought.

By studying the Septuagint and the Greek New Testament together, we also gain a deeper appreciation for the continuity and diversity within the biblical tradition. The Septuagint preserves ancient Jewish interpretations that might otherwise be lost, while the New Testament reflects the emerging Christian perspectives that built upon these foundations. This dual witness enriches our understanding of the Bible's multifaceted nature and its capacity to speak to diverse audiences across different historical and cultural contexts.

The study of the Septuagint and the Greek New Testament together is crucial for a comprehensive understanding of biblical history, theology, and textual development. This book seeks to illuminate the profound connections between these ancient scriptures, providing readers with a richer appreciation of their enduring significance. By exploring the origins, canon, textual variations, and theological implications of these texts, we can uncover the intricate tapestry of beliefs and interpretations that have shaped the Judeo-Christian tradition. This exploration not only enhances our knowledge of the Bible but also deepens our appreciation for its profound spiritual heritage.

Chapter 1

Origins of the Septuagint

Historical Background

The historical context in which the Septuagint was translated is both complex and fascinating. The translation project took place in Alexandria, Egypt, during the third and second centuries BCE, a period marked by the Hellenistic influence that followed the conquests of Alexander the Great. Alexandria was a major center of learning and culture, home to the famous Library of Alexandria and a vibrant Jewish community. The city was a melting pot of various cultures and languages, with Greek serving as the lingua franca of the eastern Mediterranean. This cosmopolitan environment necessitated a Greek translation of the Hebrew scriptures to accommodate the needs of Greek-speaking Jews who were no longer fluent in Hebrew or Aramaic.

The Jewish community in Alexandria was substantial and influential, enjoying certain privileges and integrating into the broader Hellenistic society while maintaining their religious identity. However, as generations passed, many Jews became more assimilated into Greek culture, resulting in a diminished proficiency in their ancestral languages. This linguistic shift posed a significant challenge for Jews who sought to remain faithful to their religious traditions and the study of their sacred texts. The need for a Greek translation of the Hebrew scriptures became evident to ensure that the Jewish faith could be preserved and understood within the Hellenistic context.

The translation of the Hebrew scriptures into Greek, known as the Septuagint, is traditionally attributed to a group of seventy or seventy-two Jewish scholars, hence the name "Septuagint," derived from the Latin word for seventy. According to the Letter of Aristeas, a pseudepigraphal document from the second century BCE, the translation project was initiated by Ptolemy II Philadelphus, the Greek ruler of Egypt, who sought to include the Jewish scriptures in the Library of Alexandria. He purportedly commissioned seventy-two Jewish elders, six from each of the twelve tribes of Israel, to undertake the translation. While the historical accuracy of this account is debated, it reflects the perceived importance and prestige of the translation endeavor.

The motivation behind the translation of the Hebrew scriptures into Greek was multifaceted. For the Jewish community in Alexandria, the primary impetus was to make their sacred texts accessible to Greek-speaking Jews who could no longer read Hebrew. This translation allowed them to continue practicing their faith, studying their scriptures, and participating in religious rituals. It also enabled them to engage with the broader intellectual and cultural currents of the Hellenistic world, thereby preserving their religious identity in a foreign milieu.

Furthermore, the Greek translation served as a valuable tool for proselytism and apologetics. By translating their scriptures into the dominant language of the time, Jews could communicate their religious beliefs and practices to non-Jews, fostering a better understanding of Judaism among the Hellenistic population. This translation also provided a means to defend Jewish beliefs against the criticisms and misconceptions of the Greco-Roman world, demonstrating the richness and antiquity of their religious heritage.

The translation of the Hebrew scriptures into Greek had profound implications for the development of early Christianity. The Septuagint became the primary scripture for many early Christians, including the authors of the New Testament. When the New Testament writers quoted the Old Testament, they often did so from the Septuagint rather than the Hebrew text, reflecting the widespread use and acceptance of the Greek translation among Greek-speaking Jews and Christians. This preference for the Septuagint highlights its influence on early Christian thought and its perceived authority in the early church.

In addition to its practical utility, the Septuagint's translation choices and interpretative renderings often provided unique theological insights. The translators, while striving to remain faithful to the original Hebrew, also made interpretive decisions that reflected their understanding of the text and their theological context. These choices sometimes resulted in significant differences from the Hebrew text, offering a distinct perspective on certain passages. For instance, the Septuagint's translation of Isaiah 7:14 uses the Greek word "parthenos," meaning "virgin," which early Christians interpreted as a prophecy of the virgin birth of Jesus, while the Hebrew text uses "almah," meaning "young woman." Such differences can shed light on how ancient Jewish communities understood their scriptures and how these interpretations influenced early Christian theology.

The Septuagint's influence extended beyond its immediate religious context, contributing to the broader intellectual and cultural milieu of the Hellenistic world. It provided Greek-speaking Jews and Christians with a common scriptural foundation, facilitating dialogue and interaction between different religious communities. The accessibility of the Septuagint also allowed for a richer exchange of theological and philosophical ideas, as it bridged the gap between Jewish and Greco-Roman cultures.

The translation of the Septuagint was not merely a linguistic exercise but a profound cultural and religious endeavor. It represented an effort to preserve and transmit the sacred traditions of the Jewish people in a rapidly changing world. The translators' work ensured that the Jewish scriptures could continue to speak to successive generations of Jews and, eventually, Christians, even as they navigated the complexities of living in a multicultural and multilingual society.

Understanding the historical context in which the Septuagint was translated, the motivations behind its creation, and the identity of its translators is crucial for appreciating its significance. The Septuagint was more than a simple translation; it was a monumental effort to bridge the linguistic and cultural divide between the Hebrew scriptures and the Hellenistic world. Its impact on early Christianity, its role in shaping theological thought, and its enduring influence on biblical interpretation are testaments to its profound importance in the history of religious texts.

Translation Process

The translation of the Hebrew scriptures into Greek, known as the Septuagint, was a monumental undertaking that involved a complex and methodical process. The project took place in Alexandria, Egypt, during the third and second centuries BCE, a period characterized by Hellenistic influence and the coexistence of diverse cultures and languages. The translation process, while not entirely documented in detail, can be pieced together through historical accounts, traditions, and scholarly analysis.

The translation process began with the selection of translators. According to the Letter of Aristeas, which provides a traditional but somewhat embellished account, Ptolemy II Philadelphus, the Greek ruler of Egypt, commissioned the translation to include the Jewish scriptures in the Library of Alexandria. He purportedly appointed seventy-two Jewish elders, six from each of the twelve tribes of Israel, to undertake the task. These translators were chosen for their expertise in both Hebrew and Greek, ensuring that they could accurately convey the meaning of the Hebrew scriptures in the Greek language.

The first known phase of the translation focused on the Torah, the first five books of the Hebrew Bible. This phase was likely completed around the mid-third century BCE. The translation of the Torah laid the foundation for subsequent translations of other books of the Hebrew Bible, which were completed over the next century. The entire process involved meticulous attention to linguistic nuances, cultural contexts, and theological concepts to preserve the integrity and sacredness of the original texts.

One of the primary challenges faced by the translators was the linguistic disparity between Hebrew and Greek. Hebrew, a Semitic language, has a different structure, vocabulary, and syntax compared to Greek, an Indo-European language. This linguistic gap posed significant difficulties in finding equivalent expressions and maintaining the subtleties and nuances of the original Hebrew text. The translators had to navigate these differences carefully, often making interpretative decisions to convey the intended meaning.

Another challenge was the cultural and theological context in which the translation occurred. The Hebrew scriptures were deeply rooted in the Jewish religious and cultural milieu, with concepts and practices that were foreign to the Greek-speaking Hellenistic world. The translators had to bridge this cultural divide, making the scriptures comprehensible and relevant to a new audience without compromising their religious significance. This required a deep understanding of both Jewish traditions and Hellenistic thought.

The translators also faced the issue of textual variations. The Hebrew Bible existed in multiple manuscript traditions, with variations in wording, spelling, and even content. Deciding which version of the Hebrew text to use as the basis for the translation was a critical task. The translators had to reconcile these differences and produce a coherent and authoritative Greek version. This task was complicated by the lack of a standardized Hebrew text, which would only come later with the development of the Masoretic Text.

One notable challenge was the translation of specific theological terms and concepts. For example, translating the Hebrew word "Torah" into Greek required careful consideration. The term "Torah" encompasses the notions of law, instruction, and guidance, and the

Greek word "nomos" (law) was chosen as the equivalent. However, "nomos" did not fully capture the breadth of meaning of "Torah," reflecting only the legalistic aspect and potentially missing the instructional and covenantal dimensions. Such challenges required the translators to balance fidelity to the original text with the need to communicate effectively in Greek.

The translation process also involved collaborative efforts and consultations among the translators. According to the Letter of Aristeas, the seventy-two elders worked independently at first but later compared their translations and resolved any discrepancies through discussion and consensus. This collaborative approach helped ensure the accuracy and consistency of the translation, although it also introduced the potential for interpretive biases and compromises.

Furthermore, the political and social context of the Hellenistic world presented additional challenges. The Jewish community in Alexandria, while influential and respected, had to navigate their minority status within a predominantly Greek-speaking and polytheistic society. The translation of their sacred scriptures into Greek was both an opportunity and a risk, as it exposed their religious texts to a broader audience while also subjecting them to potential misinterpretation and criticism.

Despite these challenges, the translators succeeded in producing a Greek version of the Hebrew scriptures that became widely accepted and influential. The Septuagint was not only used by Greek-speaking Jews but also became the primary scripture for early Christians, who saw it as authoritative and inspired. Its impact on the development of Christian theology and its role in the formation of the New Testament canon attest to the success and significance of the translation process.

The translation of the Septuagint involved a complex and methodical process characterized by linguistic, cultural, and theological challenges. The translators had to navigate the linguistic disparities between Hebrew and Greek, bridge cultural divides, reconcile textual variations, and make interpretative decisions to convey the meaning of the original Hebrew text. Their collaborative efforts and deep understanding of both Jewish traditions and Hellenistic thought enabled them to produce a Greek version of the Hebrew scriptures that has had a lasting impact on religious traditions and biblical scholarship.

Chapter 2

The Canon and Text of the Septuagint

Books Included

The Septuagint, a Greek translation of the Hebrew Bible, includes a collection of books that align largely with the Hebrew Bible but also contains additional writings not found in the traditional Jewish canon. This inclusion of extra texts is one of the key differences between the Septuagint and the Hebrew Bible, influencing the development of biblical canons in both Judaism and Christianity. The Septuagint comprises the Pentateuch (Genesis, Exodus, Leviticus, Numbers, Deuteronomy), which forms the Torah or the Law, and these books are common to both the Septuagint and the Hebrew Bible. The Historical Books include Joshua, Judges, Ruth, 1 Samuel, 2 Samuel, 1 Kings, 2 Kings, 1 Chronicles, 2 Chronicles, Ezra, Nehemiah, Tobit, Judith, Esther, 1 Maccabees, 2 Maccabees, and sometimes 3 Maccabees. The inclusion of Tobit, Judith, and the books of Maccabees distinguishes the Septuagint from the Hebrew Bible.

Wisdom Literature in the Septuagint includes Job, Psalms, Proverbs, Ecclesiastes, Song of Solomon, Wisdom of Solomon, and Sirach (Ecclesiasticus), with the Wisdom of Solomon and Sirach not found in the Hebrew Bible. The Prophetic Books comprise Isaiah, Jeremiah, Lamentations, Baruch, Ezekiel, Daniel, and the Twelve Minor Prophets (Hosea, Joel, Amos, Obadiah, Jonah, Micah, Nahum, Habakkuk, Zephaniah, Haggai, Zechariah, Malachi). The Book of Baruch and additions to Daniel, such as the Prayer of Azariah and the Song of the Three Holy Children, Susanna, and Bel and the Dragon, are unique to the Septuagint. The additional books and additions within certain books, such as Daniel and Esther, reflect the broader literary and theological traditions within Hellenistic Judaism. These texts provide insights into Jewish thought and practice during the Hellenistic period and have significantly impacted Christian biblical canons.

The variations between the Septuagint and the Hebrew Bible are not limited to the inclusion of additional books. There are also notable textual differences and variations within the books common to both canons. These differences often arise from the translation process and the diverse manuscript traditions that existed. Significant variations in the Septuagint include differences in wording, order, and content. For example, the Book of Jeremiah in the Septuagint is significantly shorter than in the Hebrew Bible, with different arrangement of sections. Similarly, the Psalms in the Septuagint occasionally differ in numbering and sometimes contain additional material not found in the Hebrew text.

Manuscripts of the Septuagint also show a range of textual traditions, reflecting the complex transmission history of the text. Key manuscripts include Codex Vaticanus (B), dating from the fourth century CE, one of the oldest and most complete extant copies of the Septuagint. It contains most of the Old Testament and some New Testament texts, with notable gaps. Codex Sinaiticus (S), also from the fourth century CE, includes a large portion of the Septuagint and the New Testament, along with some apocryphal works. Its significance lies in its completeness and early date. Codex Alexandrinus (A), dating from the fifth century CE, contains a nearly complete Septuagint and New Testament. It provides important textual variants and is a critical source for textual criticism. Codex Ephraemi Rescriptus (C), a fifth-century manuscript, is a palimpsest, meaning the original biblical text was partially erased and overwritten with other writings. It still offers valuable insights into the Septuagint's textual history. Codex Bezae (D), primarily known for its New Testament text, also contains fragments of the Septuagint, particularly the Pentateuch. It provides a unique Western text-type perspective.

Textual variations among these manuscripts highlight the fluidity and diversity of the Septuagint text over time. Scholars use these variations to reconstruct the most likely original text and understand the development and transmission of the Septuagint. The differences between the Septuagint and the Hebrew Bible have significant implications for biblical interpretation and theology. The

Septuagint's unique readings and additional books have shaped Christian doctrine and practice, particularly in the Eastern Orthodox and Roman Catholic traditions, which include these texts in their canons. Theological concepts such as the Virgin Birth and the Messianic expectations in Christianity are influenced by the Septuagint's renderings of key passages.

The study of the Septuagint also involves textual criticism, the scholarly discipline of analyzing and comparing manuscripts to determine the most accurate text. Textual criticism of the Septuagint is particularly challenging due to the variety of manuscript traditions and the historical context of its translation. Scholars must consider the linguistic, cultural, and theological factors that influenced the translators' choices and the subsequent transmission of the text. One significant aspect of textual criticism is the examination of the Hexapla, an ancient critical edition of the Old Testament compiled by the early Christian scholar Origen in the third century CE. The Hexapla presented the Hebrew text, a transliteration of the Hebrew into Greek characters, and several Greek translations, including the Septuagint, in parallel columns. This work aimed to compare and evaluate different textual traditions, highlighting the diversity and complexity of the biblical text.

The discovery of the Dead Sea Scrolls in the mid-20th century provided additional insights into the textual history of the Septuagint. These ancient manuscripts, which include fragments of the Septuagint, have helped scholars understand the relationship between the Septuagint and the Hebrew Bible and have shed light on the textual variations and developments within both traditions. The Septuagint includes a range of books that extend beyond the traditional Jewish canon, reflecting the broader literary and theological traditions of Hellenistic Judaism. The significant variations between the Septuagint and the Hebrew Bible, as well as the diversity of manuscript traditions, highlight the complexity of the translation process and the transmission history of the text. The study of the Septuagint through textual criticism and the examination of key manuscripts offers valuable insights into the development of biblical texts and their enduring impact on religious traditions and biblical scholarship.

Variations and Manuscripts

The criteria for determining the inclusion of books in the Septuagint were influenced by a combination of religious, cultural, linguistic, and historical factors. Understanding these criteria provides insight into the broader context in which the Septuagint was produced and its significance for both Jewish and early Christian communities.

One primary criterion was the religious significance of the texts to the Jewish community in Alexandria, Egypt, where the translation was initiated. The books included in the Septuagint were those considered sacred and authoritative by the Jewish population there. This community had a strong connection to the Temple in Jerusalem and adhered to Jewish religious practices, thus the texts chosen for translation reflected their religious traditions and beliefs.

The historical context of Hellenistic Judaism played a significant role in the selection of books. During the Hellenistic period, Jewish communities were spread throughout the Mediterranean world, and many Jews had become Greek-speaking due to the widespread influence of Greek culture and language following the conquests of Alexander the Great. The need to preserve and transmit Jewish religious traditions in a language accessible to these communities was a crucial factor. Books that were central to Jewish religious life and thought were prioritized for translation to ensure that Greek-speaking Jews could maintain their religious identity and heritage.

Linguistic considerations were also important. The translators needed to choose texts that could be effectively rendered into Greek. Some books, due to their language, style, or content, may have been more amenable to translation than others. The translators aimed to produce a text that was both faithful to the original Hebrew and understandable to Greek readers, balancing literal accuracy with readability.

The theological and moral teachings of the books were another criterion. Texts that conveyed essential aspects of Jewish law, ethics, and theology were included to provide a comprehensive guide to Jewish life and belief. The Pentateuch, with its foundational narratives and laws, was central to this effort, as were the Prophetic books and Wisdom literature, which offered guidance and reflection on living a righteous life in accordance with God's will.

The influence of Jewish oral traditions and interpretations also played a role. The Septuagint translators were not working in isolation but were part of a broader Jewish scholarly tradition. The texts selected for translation often reflected contemporary Jewish interpretations and expansions of biblical stories and laws. Books that were widely read, discussed, and interpreted in Jewish communities were more likely to be included.

Cultural and political considerations of the time influenced the selection as well. The translation project was undertaken under the patronage of the Ptolemaic rulers of Egypt, who supported the inclusion of Jewish texts in the Library of Alexandria. This political support may have influenced the selection of texts that were seen as important for preserving Jewish culture and history in a Hellenistic context.

The process was also shaped by practical considerations, such as the availability of Hebrew manuscripts and the expertise of the translators. The books included in the Septuagint were those for which accurate and complete Hebrew texts were available and for which there were scholars capable of translating them into Greek. This practical aspect ensured that the translation project could proceed efficiently and produce a coherent and authoritative text.

Over time, the inclusion of certain books in the Septuagint was also validated by their use and acceptance within Jewish and Christian communities. The liturgical use of these texts, their citation in religious teachings and writings, and their role in shaping religious thought contributed to their enduring place in the Septuagint canon.

The criteria for the inclusion of books in the Septuagint were multifaceted, encompassing religious significance, historical context, linguistic feasibility, theological and moral content, influence of Jewish oral traditions, cultural and political considerations, practical availability of manuscripts, and validation through community acceptance and use. These factors combined to produce a text that was both faithful to Jewish religious traditions and accessible to Greek-speaking Jewish and Christian communities, ensuring the preservation and transmission of sacred writings across different cultural and linguistic contexts.

Chapter 3

The Influence of the Septuagint in Hellenistic Judaism

Jewish Diaspora and the Septuagint

The Jewish Diaspora, the dispersion of Jews beyond Israel, played a critical role in the use and spread of the Septuagint. As Jews settled in various parts of the Mediterranean and Near East, they encountered different languages and cultures, necessitating adaptations to maintain their religious identity and traditions. The Septuagint, a Greek translation of the Hebrew scriptures, emerged as a vital tool in this context.

The primary factor contributing to the widespread use of the Septuagint was the linguistic shift among Jews living in Hellenistic territories. Greek had become the lingua franca of the Eastern Mediterranean and Near East after the conquests of Alexander the Great. Many Jews, especially those in Alexandria, Egypt, had adopted Greek as their primary language, resulting in a gradual decline in their ability to understand Hebrew. The Septuagint enabled these Greek-speaking Jews to access their sacred texts in a language they understood, preserving their religious heritage in the face of linguistic change.

The Jewish communities in Alexandria, one of the largest and most influential centers of the Jewish Diaspora, were particularly instrumental in the creation and dissemination of the Septuagint. Alexandria was a hub of Hellenistic culture and learning, and its Jewish population was well-integrated into the broader society while maintaining their distinct religious identity. The production of the Septuagint in Alexandria, under the patronage of Ptolemaic rulers, was driven by the need to include Jewish scriptures in the famous Library of Alexandria, as well as to meet the religious needs of the local Jewish community. This translation provided a means for Jews to engage with their scriptures in the context of a dominant Greek culture.

As the Septuagint gained acceptance among Greek-speaking Jews, its influence extended beyond Alexandria to other parts of the Jewish Diaspora. Jewish communities in cities such as Antioch, Ephesus, and Rome, where Greek was widely spoken, adopted the Septuagint for religious study and worship. This widespread adoption was facilitated by the interconnectedness of these communities through trade, travel, and communication networks. The use of the Septuagint in synagogues and private study helped ensure that Jewish religious practices and beliefs remained cohesive despite geographical dispersion.

The Septuagint also played a crucial role in the religious life of the Jewish Diaspora by providing a common scriptural foundation. In the diverse and often fragmented context of the Diaspora, the Septuagint served as a unifying text that helped maintain a sense of shared identity and continuity among Jewish communities. This was especially important in the absence of the central Temple in Jerusalem, as the Septuagint enabled Jews to observe their religious traditions and teachings wherever they were.

The spread of the Septuagint was further enhanced by its use in Jewish liturgy and education. Greek-speaking synagogues adopted the Septuagint for public readings and interpretations of scripture, ensuring that congregants could understand the texts being read. Additionally, Jewish educators and scholars used the Septuagint to teach younger generations, who were often more fluent in Greek than Hebrew, about their religious heritage. This educational use of the Septuagint helped embed it deeply within the cultural and religious life of the Diaspora.

The significance of the Septuagint was not limited to Jewish communities; it also had a profound impact on early Christianity. The early Christians, many of whom were Greek-speaking Jews or Gentiles, adopted the Septuagint as their primary scriptural text. The New Testament writers frequently quoted from the Septuagint, and its Greek translations of messianic prophecies and other key passages influenced the development of Christian theology. The use of the Septuagint by early Christians further contributed to its spread and preservation, as it became integral to the formation of the Christian biblical canon.

The theological and interpretive choices made by the Septuagint translators also resonated with the broader Hellenistic context, making the text more accessible to non-Jewish audiences. The translators often rendered Hebrew idioms and concepts into terms that were comprehensible to Greek speakers, facilitating cross-cultural understanding. This adaptability helped the Septuagint reach a wider audience, including Hellenistic Jews and early Christians who were navigating the complexities of living in a multicultural and multilingual environment.

The Jewish Diaspora's role in the spread of the Septuagint was also shaped by the geopolitical and social dynamics of the time. The Diaspora communities were often situated in cosmopolitan cities that were centers of trade and cultural exchange. This strategic positioning allowed for the diffusion of the Septuagint through commercial and social interactions. Jewish merchants, travelers, and scholars carried copies of the Septuagint to various regions, where it was adopted by local communities and integrated into their religious practices.

The translation of the Hebrew scriptures into Greek also reflected a broader trend of cultural adaptation and integration within the Jewish Diaspora. The Hellenistic period was characterized by a blending of cultures, and the Septuagint is an example of how Jewish religious texts were adapted to fit this new cultural milieu. By translating their sacred texts into Greek, Jews were able to preserve their religious identity while engaging with the dominant culture of their time. This adaptability was crucial for the survival and flourishing of Jewish communities in the Diaspora.

Moreover, the Septuagint's influence extended to the realm of biblical scholarship and textual criticism. The Greek translation provided a valuable reference point for scholars studying the Hebrew Bible and its transmission. The differences between the Septuagint and the Hebrew Masoretic Text, such as variations in wording, order, and content, have been subjects of scholarly inquiry, shedding light on the history of the biblical text and its interpretation. The Septuagint's role in the textual history of the Bible underscores its significance as a key document in both Jewish and Christian traditions.

The translation addressed the linguistic needs of Greek-speaking Jews, preserving their religious identity in a Hellenistic context. The widespread adoption of the Septuagint in Diaspora communities helped maintain religious cohesion and continuity. Its use in liturgy, education, and early Christianity further contributed to its dissemination. The Septuagint's adaptability to Hellenistic culture facilitated its acceptance by a broader audience, including non-Jews. The geopolitical and social dynamics of the Diaspora, along with the strategic positioning of Jewish communities in cosmopolitan centers, enabled the diffusion of the Septuagint through commercial and social interactions. The Septuagint also played a significant role in biblical scholarship and textual criticism, providing a valuable reference point for studying the Hebrew Bible. Through these multifaceted contributions, the Jewish Diaspora ensured that the Septuagint became a foundational text for both Jewish and Christian traditions, influencing religious thought and practice across different cultures and languages.

Use in Jewish Worship

The Septuagint, as a Greek translation of the Hebrew scriptures, held a significant place in Jewish worship and community life, especially for those living outside Israel. Its use extended beyond mere translation, becoming a bridge that connected the Jewish diaspora to their religious roots and traditions.

In Jewish worship, the Septuagint was instrumental in public readings and liturgical practices within synagogues. Greek-speaking Jews, who were no longer fluent in Hebrew, relied on the Septuagint to understand and engage with their sacred texts. During synagogue services, scriptures were read aloud, and the Septuagint provided an accessible version of these readings, ensuring that the congregation could comprehend the lessons and commandments being imparted. This practice reinforced religious teachings and maintained the continuity of Jewish worship across different linguistic landscapes.

It served as a primary text for teaching young Jews about their heritage, laws, and traditions. Parents and teachers used the Septuagint to instruct children in the stories and commandments of their faith, making religious education accessible to those who spoke Greek. This ensured that the new generation could carry forward the Jewish faith and identity, even in a predominantly Greek-speaking environment.

Beyond worship and education, the Septuagint was central to the daily religious practices and community life of Jews in the diaspora. It was used in personal study and reflection, allowing individuals to engage with their faith on a deeper level. The availability of the scriptures in Greek meant that Jews could read and meditate on their sacred texts at home, fostering a personal connection to their religion. This personal engagement was crucial in sustaining the faith of individuals and families in a foreign cultural context.

For Jews living outside of Israel, the Septuagint held immense significance as a symbol of their religious identity and continuity. It allowed them to remain connected to their ancestral traditions while adapting to their new cultural surroundings. The translation was not just a linguistic shift but a cultural adaptation that enabled Jews to navigate the complexities of living in a Hellenistic world. By preserving their scriptures in a widely understood language, Jews could maintain their distinct religious identity amidst the dominant Greek culture.

The Septuagint also facilitated the interaction between Jewish and non-Jewish communities. Greek was the common language of the Mediterranean world, and having the Hebrew scriptures translated into Greek made them accessible to a broader audience. This accessibility fostered a greater understanding and respect for Jewish traditions among non-Jews, and it opened avenues for religious and philosophical dialogues. The presence of the Septuagint in public libraries and its use in scholarly discussions highlighted the intellectual and cultural contributions of the Jewish community to the wider Hellenistic world.

The translation of the Hebrew scriptures into Greek also had theological implications for Jews in the diaspora. The Septuagint provided interpretations and nuances that were influenced by the cultural and philosophical context of Hellenistic society. This interaction enriched Jewish theological thought and allowed Jews to express their faith in ways that resonated with their new environment. The Septuagint's influence is evident in the writings of Jewish philosophers like Philo of Alexandria, who used Greek philosophical concepts to articulate Jewish theology.

Furthermore, the Septuagint's role extended to the realm of legal and moral instruction. The translation included the laws and commandments of the Hebrew Bible, making them accessible to Greek-speaking Jews. This was particularly important for maintaining the moral and ethical standards of the Jewish community. The Septuagint served as a reference for legal decisions and ethical guidance, ensuring that Jewish law remained a living and applicable force in the daily lives of Jews in the diaspora.

The significance of the Septuagint for Jews outside of Israel was also reflected in its impact on community cohesion. The translation provided a shared scriptural foundation that united diverse Jewish communities across different regions. Despite geographical and cultural differences, the Septuagint allowed Jews to practice their faith in a unified manner. This cohesion was crucial for preserving Jewish identity and solidarity in a diaspora that spanned vast and varied territories.

The Septuagint's influence extended to the preservation and transmission of Jewish liturgical traditions. Many of the psalms and hymns used in worship were translated into Greek, enabling Greek-speaking Jews to participate fully in liturgical practices. This translation of liturgical texts helped to maintain the richness and depth of Jewish worship, ensuring that the spiritual and emotional aspects of the faith were preserved in the new linguistic context.

The use of the Septuagint also had eschatological significance for Jews in the diaspora. The translation included prophetic texts that spoke of the future restoration of Israel and the coming of the Messiah. These prophecies provided hope and encouragement to Jews living in exile, reminding them of God's promises and sustaining their faith in difficult times. The Septuagint thus served as a source of spiritual strength and consolation for Jews awaiting the fulfillment of divine promises.

Moreover, the Septuagint played a vital role in the transmission of Jewish wisdom literature. Books such as Proverbs, Ecclesiastes, and the Wisdom of Solomon were translated into Greek, making their teachings available to a wider audience. This wisdom literature provided practical and philosophical guidance for living a righteous life, and its translation into Greek allowed these teachings to influence both Jewish and Hellenistic thought.

The Septuagint's significance also extended to its role in shaping early Christian theology and scripture. The early Christians, many of whom were Greek-speaking Jews or Gentiles, adopted the Septuagint as their primary scriptural text. The New Testament writers frequently quoted from the Septuagint, and its Greek translations of messianic prophecies and other key passages influenced the development of Christian doctrine. The use of the Septuagint by early Christians further contributed to its spread and preservation, as it became integral to the formation of the Christian biblical canon.

Theological concepts such as the Virgin Birth and the Messianic expectations in Christianity were influenced by the Septuagint's renderings of key passages. For instance, the Septuagint's translation of Isaiah 7:14 uses the Greek word "parthenos" (virgin) rather than the Hebrew "almah" (young woman), shaping the Christian interpretation of the prophecy concerning the birth of Jesus. This and other translations played a significant role in the theological debates and developments of early Christianity.

The Septuagint also had a profound impact on the development of biblical hermeneutics and exegesis. Jewish and Christian scholars alike used the Greek text for scriptural interpretation, leading to rich traditions of commentary and theological reflection. The differences between the Septuagint and the Hebrew Masoretic Text, such as variations in wording, order, and content, became subjects of scholarly inquiry, shedding light on the history of the biblical text and its interpretation.

The presence of the Septuagint in various Jewish communities contributed to the broader cultural and intellectual exchanges of the Hellenistic world. The translation was included in the famous Library of Alexandria, reflecting the integration of Jewish thought into the wider cultural milieu. This integration highlighted the contributions of Jewish scholarship to the broader intellectual landscape and facilitated the preservation of Jewish texts for future generations.

The Septuagint's role in Jewish worship and community life, coupled with its significance for Jews living outside of Israel, underscores its profound impact on religious and cultural history. It enabled Greek-speaking Jews to maintain their religious identity, fostered community cohesion, and facilitated theological and intellectual exchanges. Through its use in worship, education, legal and moral instruction, and personal study, the Septuagint ensured that Jewish traditions and beliefs were preserved and transmitted across generations and cultural boundaries. Its influence extended beyond the Jewish community, shaping early Christian theology and contributing to the rich tapestry of religious thought in the Hellenistic world. The Septuagint remains a testament to the enduring resilience and adaptability of the Jewish faith and its ability to thrive in diverse and changing environments.

Chapter 4

The Septuagint in Early Christianity

Quotations in the New Testament

The New Testament is replete with quotations and allusions to the Septuagint, reflecting its profound influence on early Christian thought and theology. These quotations serve to bridge the Old and New Testaments, highlighting the continuity of divine revelation and the fulfillment of prophecies in the person of Jesus Christ. Notable quotations from the Septuagint in the New Testament provide crucial theological insights and establish the foundation for key Christian doctrines.

One significant quotation of the Septuagint is found in Matthew 1:23, which cites Isaiah 7:14. In the Septuagint, Isaiah 7:14 reads, "Behold, the virgin shall conceive and bear a son, and they shall call his name Immanuel." The Greek term "parthenos," meaning "virgin," is used instead of the Hebrew term "almah," which can mean "young woman." This translation choice in the Septuagint underscores the miraculous nature of Jesus' birth and affirms the virgin birth as a fulfillment of Old Testament prophecy. Matthew's use of this passage in the context of Jesus' nativity emphasizes the divine intervention and the fulfillment of God's promise to dwell among His people.

Another notable quotation is found in Hebrews 1:6, which references Deuteronomy 32:43. The Septuagint version of Deuteronomy includes the phrase, "Let all the angels of God worship Him," which is not present in the Masoretic Text. Hebrews 1:6 uses this quotation to assert the superiority of Christ over the angels, reinforcing His divine nature and preeminence. This usage highlights the theological importance of the Septuagint in articulating the divinity of Christ and His exalted status in the heavenly realm.

In Romans 3:10-18, Paul quotes several passages from the Septuagint to illustrate the universality of sin and the need for divine grace. This composite quotation includes references to Psalms 14:1-3, 5:9, 140:3, and Isaiah 59:7-8. The Septuagint's wording in these passages is slightly different from the Hebrew text, emphasizing the comprehensive depravity of humanity. Paul's use of these quotations underscores the consistent biblical theme of human sinfulness and the necessity of salvation through Christ.

The book of Acts also contains numerous quotations from the Septuagint, reflecting its centrality in the preaching and teaching of the early church. In Acts 2:17-21, Peter quotes Joel 2:28-32 from the Septuagint during his Pentecost sermon. The passage speaks of the outpouring of the Holy Spirit in the last days, accompanied by prophetic visions and signs. The Septuagint's rendering of this prophecy emphasizes the inclusivity of the Spirit's outpouring, extending to "all flesh," including both Jews and Gentiles. Peter's use of this passage highlights the fulfillment of Joel's prophecy in the events of Pentecost and the inauguration of the new covenant community.

In Galatians 3:13, Paul cites Deuteronomy 21:23 from the Septuagint to explain the redemptive work of Christ. The Septuagint version of Deuteronomy states, "Cursed is everyone who hangs on a tree." Paul uses this quotation to elucidate how Christ, by being crucified, took upon Himself the curse of the law on behalf of humanity. This theological interpretation underscores the sacrificial nature of Christ's death and its significance in liberating believers from the curse of sin and the law.

The use of the Septuagint in the New Testament extends to the book of Revelation, where John frequently draws upon its imagery and language. In Revelation 1:7, John quotes Zechariah 12:10 from the Septuagint: "They will look on Him whom they have pierced." This quotation is used to depict the eschatological return of Christ and the recognition of His messianic identity by all peoples. The Septuagint's rendering of Zechariah's prophecy emphasizes the visible and public nature of Christ's second coming, reinforcing the themes of judgment and redemption.

In the Gospel of John, Jesus Himself quotes the Septuagint. In John 10:34, Jesus references Psalm 82:6, saying, "Is it not written in your law, 'I said, you are gods'?" The Septuagint version of this Psalm speaks of God's declaration to the judges of Israel, and Jesus uses this passage to defend His claim to divinity. By quoting the Septuagint, Jesus appeals to the authority of the scriptures familiar to His audience, demonstrating His intimate knowledge of the texts and their deeper theological implications.

The apostle Peter, in his first epistle, quotes Isaiah 40:6-8 from the Septuagint in 1 Peter 1:24-25: "All flesh is like grass, and all its glory like the flower of grass. The grass withers, and the flower falls, but the word of the Lord remains forever." The Septuagint's version of Isaiah emphasizes the transient nature of human life contrasted with the enduring word of God. Peter uses this quotation to encourage believers to trust in the eternal promises of God amidst the trials and persecutions they face.

Another profound use of the Septuagint is found in the book of Hebrews, particularly in Hebrews 10:5-7, which quotes Psalm 40:6-8. The Septuagint version of this Psalm reads, "Sacrifice and offering You did not desire, but a body You have prepared for Me." This differs from the Hebrew text, which speaks of God opening ears instead of preparing a body. The Septuagint's wording underscores the incarnation of Christ, who offered Himself as the ultimate sacrifice. This quotation highlights the fulfillment of Old Testament sacrificial themes in the person and work of Jesus, emphasizing His obedience and submission to the Father's will.

In Matthew 21:16, Jesus quotes Psalm 8:2 from the Septuagint in response to the chief priests and scribes: "Out of the mouth of infants and nursing babies you have prepared praise." The Septuagint's rendering emphasizes the spontaneous and pure praise offered by children, contrasting with the skepticism of the religious leaders. Jesus' use of this quotation highlights the acceptance and recognition of His messianic role by the humble and innocent, fulfilling the prophetic vision of divine praise.

Paul, in his epistle to the Ephesians, quotes Psalm 68:18 from the Septuagint in Ephesians 4:8: "When He ascended on high, He led captivity captive and gave gifts to men." The Septuagint's version of this Psalm depicts the victorious ascent of a conqueror distributing spoils. Paul applies this imagery to Christ's ascension and the subsequent outpouring of spiritual gifts to the church. This quotation underscores the triumph of Christ over sin and death and His generosity in bestowing gifts upon His followers.

The influence of the Septuagint on the New Testament writers is further evident in Paul's epistle to the Romans, particularly in Romans 15:12, where he quotes Isaiah 11:10 from the Septuagint: "There shall come the root of Jesse, and He who arises to rule over the Gentiles, in Him shall the Gentiles hope." The Septuagint's rendering emphasizes the messianic hope and the inclusion of the Gentiles in God's salvific plan. Paul uses this quotation to affirm the universal scope of the gospel and the fulfillment of God's promises to the nations through Christ.

The book of Acts also records Stephen's speech before the Sanhedrin, where he quotes extensively from the Septuagint. In Acts 7:14, Stephen cites Genesis 46:27, saying, "And Joseph sent and summoned Jacob his father and all his kindred, seventy-five persons in all." The Septuagint's version includes a different number of Jacob's descendants compared to the Hebrew text, reflecting a variant tradition. Stephen's use of the Septuagint in his speech demonstrates its authority and acceptance within the early Christian community and serves to connect their faith with the broader Jewish scriptural tradition.

In Galatians 4:27, Paul quotes Isaiah 54:1 from the Septuagint: "Rejoice, O barren one who does not bear; break forth and shout, you who are not in labor! For the children of the desolate one will be more than those of the one who has a husband." The Septuagint's rendering of this prophecy emphasizes the miraculous and abundant blessings bestowed upon the desolate woman, symbolizing the inclusion of the Gentiles and the expansion of God's covenant community. Paul uses this quotation to illustrate the fulfillment of God's promises and the transformative power of the gospel.

The apostle James, in his epistle, quotes Proverbs 3:34 from the Septuagint in James 4:6: "God opposes the proud but gives grace to the humble." The Septuagint's wording highlights the contrast between God's opposition to pride and His favor towards humility. James uses this quotation to exhort believers to adopt a posture of humility and dependence on God's grace, reinforcing the ethical teachings of the wisdom literature within the Christian context.

The use of the Septuagint in the New Testament also extends to the Pauline epistles. In 2 Corinthians 6:2, Paul quotes Isaiah 49:8 from the Septuagint: "In a favorable time I listened to you, and in a day of salvation I have helped you." The Septuagint's rendering underscores the timely and gracious nature of God's salvation. Paul applies this quotation to emphasize the urgency and immediacy of the gospel message, urging believers to respond to God's offer of salvation in the present moment.

The notable quotations of the Septuagint in the New Testament highlight its profound impact on early Christian theology and scriptural interpretation. These quotations underscore the continuity between the Old and New Testaments, affirm the fulfillment of messianic prophecies, and articulate key doctrinal themes such as the virgin birth,

Theological Implications

The influence of the Septuagint on early Christian thought and writings carries profound theological implications, shaping the foundational doctrines and hermeneutical approaches of the nascent Christian community. The Septuagint, as the Greek translation of the Hebrew scriptures, served as the primary scriptural text for many early Christians, particularly those in Hellenistic regions. This translation provided a vital bridge between the Jewish roots of Christianity and its expansion into the Greek-speaking world, embedding deep theological resonances into early Christian teachings and writings.

One significant theological implication of the Septuagint's influence is its role in the Christological interpretations of Old Testament prophecies. Early Christians viewed the Septuagint as a prophetic text that pointed directly to Jesus Christ. For example, the Septuagint's translation of Isaiah 7:14, "Behold, the virgin shall conceive and bear a son," is pivotal for the doctrine of the virgin birth, as cited in Matthew 1:23. The Greek term "parthenos" specifically denotes a virgin, thus providing a clear link to the miraculous birth of Jesus. This interpretation reinforced the belief in Jesus' divine nature and His fulfillment of messianic prophecies.

Furthermore, the Septuagint's rendering of various messianic passages contributed to the development of soteriological themes in early Christian theology. For instance, the translation of Isaiah 53, known as the Suffering Servant passage, provided a framework for understanding Jesus' sacrificial death. The detailed descriptions of suffering, rejection, and ultimate vindication in the Septuagint informed the theological reflections on Jesus' passion and atonement. Early Christians saw in these passages the prefiguration of Christ's redemptive work, thus affirming the continuity of God's salvific plan from the Old Testament to the New Testament.

The Septuagint also played a crucial role in the articulation of the doctrine of the Trinity. Quotations from the Septuagint that refer to divine activities and attributes were often interpreted in a Trinitarian context. For example, Psalm 110:1 in the Septuagint, "The Lord said to my Lord, 'Sit at my right hand, until I make your enemies your footstool,'" is cited in the New Testament to support the exaltation of Christ and His divine authority alongside the Father. This passage, among others, provided a scriptural basis for understanding the relational dynamics within the Godhead, reinforcing the theological foundation for the Trinity.

Early Christian eschatology was also deeply influenced by the Septuagint. The translation of prophetic books such as Daniel and Ezekiel, with their vivid apocalyptic imagery, shaped early Christian expectations of the end times. The book of Revelation, in particular, draws heavily on the language and symbolism of the

Septuagint, creating a tapestry of eschatological hope and divine judgment. The Septuagint's portrayal of future restoration and the coming of God's kingdom resonated with early Christians, who saw themselves as participants in the unfolding of these prophetic visions.

The translation of the wisdom literature, including Proverbs, Ecclesiastes, and the Wisdom of Solomon, provided a rich source of moral and philosophical guidance. The ethical precepts found in these books were integrated into Christian teachings, emphasizing virtues such as humility, wisdom, and righteousness. For instance, the Epistle of James draws extensively on the Septuagint's wisdom literature to exhort believers to live out their faith through practical and righteous actions.

The Septuagint also impacted early Christian liturgical practices. The Psalms, translated in the Septuagint, were integral to Jewish worship and were seamlessly incorporated into Christian liturgy. The use of the Psalms in prayer, hymnody, and communal worship reflected the continuity of worship practices from Judaism to Christianity. The Septuagint's poetic and accessible language facilitated its adoption in the Greek-speaking churches, enriching the spiritual life of early Christian communities.

Early Christians' view of the Septuagint compared to the Hebrew texts is a complex interplay of reverence, adaptation, and theological interpretation. The Septuagint was often considered divinely inspired and authoritative, on par with the Hebrew scriptures. This high regard is evident in the extensive use of the Septuagint in the New Testament writings, where it is frequently quoted and referenced. The early church fathers, such as Justin Martyr and Irenaeus, defended the Septuagint's authenticity and its role in revealing Christ.

However, early Christians also recognized differences between the Septuagint and the Hebrew texts, which sometimes led to theological reflections and adaptations. The variations in wording and content between the two versions were not seen as contradictions but as complementary revelations of God's word. For example, the quotation of Deuteronomy 32:43 in Hebrews 1:6, which includes the phrase "Let all the angels of God worship Him," is found in the Septuagint but not in the Masoretic Text. This variation was seen as a providential expansion that illuminated Christ's divine status.

The theological implications of the Septuagint's influence extend to the formation of the Christian biblical canon. The inclusion of the Deuterocanonical books in the Septuagint, which are absent from the Hebrew Bible, enriched the theological and spiritual landscape of early Christianity. These books, such as Wisdom of Solomon, Sirach, and 1 and 2 Maccabees, provided additional historical, ethical, and theological insights that were embraced by the early church. The Septuagint's canon thus shaped the breadth and depth of the Christian scriptural tradition.

Moreover, the adoption of the Septuagint by early Christians facilitated the spread of the gospel in the Hellenistic world. The Greek language was the lingua franca of the Eastern Mediterranean, and the Septuagint made the Jewish scriptures accessible to a wider audience. This accessibility enabled the apostles and early missionaries to proclaim the message of Jesus using a common scriptural foundation. The Septuagint's influence on the language and thought of the New Testament writers also facilitated the engagement with Greek-speaking audiences, who were familiar with the Septuagint's texts and terminology.

The early church's reliance on the Septuagint also contributed to theological debates and controversies. The differences between the Septuagint and the Hebrew texts were sometimes points of contention between Jews and Christians. For instance, the Septuagint's rendering of certain messianic prophecies was a focal point in discussions about Jesus' identity and mission. Early Christians defended the Septuagint's translations as divinely guided and reflective of the true meaning of the prophecies, while Jewish scholars often preferred the Hebrew text.

The theological implications of the Septuagint's influence are further seen in the development of Christian hermeneutics. The Septuagint provided a framework for interpreting the Old Testament in light of Christ. Typological and allegorical readings of the scriptures, which saw events, persons, and institutions in the Old Testament as foreshadowing Christ and the church, were facilitated by the Septuagint's translation choices. For example, the translation of the Hebrew word "almah" as "parthenos" (virgin) in Isaiah 7:14 was seen as a typological indication of the virgin birth of Christ.

Early Christian exegetes, such as Origen and Jerome, engaged deeply with the Septuagint in their biblical commentaries. Origen's Hexapla, a critical edition of the Old Testament that included the Hebrew text, the Septuagint, and other Greek translations, exemplifies the scholarly efforts to understand the relationship between the different textual traditions. Jerome's translation of the Bible into Latin, the Vulgate, drew from both the Hebrew and Septuagint texts, reflecting a synthesis of these traditions in the service of the church.

The Septuagint's influence also extends to the patristic writings, where the church fathers employed its language and concepts in their theological and doctrinal expositions. The writings of the early church fathers, such as Athanasius, Augustine, and Chrysostom, are replete with references to the Septuagint. These fathers used the Septuagint to articulate and defend key doctrines, such as the divinity of Christ, the nature of the Trinity, and the fulfillment of Old Testament prophecies in the New Testament.

The early Christians' view of the Septuagint compared to the Hebrew texts is encapsulated in the idea of the Septuagint as a providential and inspired translation that revealed God's truth in the language of the time. This view is articulated by Justin Martyr, who saw the Septuagint as divinely inspired and superior to the Hebrew text. Justin argued that the translation was guided by the Holy Spirit to make the scriptures accessible and comprehensible to the Greek-speaking world, thereby fulfilling God's plan of salvation.

Chapter 5

The Greek New Testament: Formation and Canon

Writing and Compilation

The process of writing and compiling the books of the New Testament is a monumental endeavor in the history of Christianity, reflecting the early church's response to the teachings of Jesus Christ and the movement He initiated. The New Testament comprises 27 books, including the Gospels, Acts of the Apostles, Pauline and General Epistles, and Revelation. These texts were written over several decades, from approximately 50 AD to 100 AD, by various authors, each inspired by the Holy Spirit to address the theological, pastoral, and eschatological needs of the burgeoning Christian communities.

The Gospels are central to the New Testament, chronicling the life, ministry, death, and resurrection of Jesus Christ. The Gospel according to Mark is widely considered the earliest, likely written around 65-70 AD. Mark's Gospel is succinct and action-oriented, emphasizing Jesus as the suffering servant and the Son of God. It is believed that Mark's account was based on the apostle Peter's teachings and recollections. The Gospel according to Matthew, written between 70-85

AD, draws heavily on Mark but adds extensive teachings of Jesus, such as the Sermon on the Mount. Matthew's Gospel aims to present Jesus as the fulfillment of Old Testament prophecies and the new Moses, establishing His role as the Messiah and King.

The Gospel according to Luke, written around 80-90 AD, is notable for its detailed historical and theological narrative. Luke, a companion of Paul and a physician, sought to provide an orderly account of Jesus' life and ministry, emphasizing His compassion, outreach to Gentiles, and the role of the Holy Spirit. Luke's Gospel, along with its sequel, the Acts of the Apostles, offers a comprehensive view of the early church's expansion and the work of the Holy Spirit in spreading the gospel. The Gospel according to John, likely written around 90-100 AD, is distinct in its theological depth and focus on Jesus' divinity. John's Gospel presents Jesus as the eternal Word (Logos) made flesh, emphasizing His pre-existence, divine nature, and the importance of belief for eternal life.

The Acts of the Apostles, authored by Luke, serves as a continuation of his Gospel, detailing the early church's history from Jesus' ascension to Paul's imprisonment in Rome. Written around 80-90 AD, Acts highlights the work of the Holy Spirit, the spread of the gospel from Jerusalem to the ends of the earth, and the inclusion of Gentiles into the Christian community. The book is structured around key figures such as Peter and Paul, demonstrating how the apostles carried out the Great

Commission and established churches throughout the Roman Empire.

The Pauline Epistles, attributed to the apostle Paul, form a substantial portion of the New Testament. These letters, written between 50-67 AD, address various theological, ethical, and pastoral issues within early Christian communities. Paul's letters, such as Romans, 1 and 2 Corinthians, Galatians, Ephesians, Philippians, Colossians, and 1 and 2 Thessalonians, provide profound insights into the doctrines of grace, justification by faith, the role of the law, the nature of the church, and the second coming of Christ. Paul's pastoral epistles, including 1 and 2 Timothy and Titus, offer guidance on church leadership, sound doctrine, and the responsibilities of Christian ministers.

The General Epistles, written by various apostles and church leaders, address broader audiences and themes within the early church. The Epistle of James, written by James, the brother of Jesus, emphasizes practical Christian living, faith and works, and the power of prayer. The Epistles of Peter (1 and 2 Peter), attributed to the apostle Peter, provide encouragement in the face of suffering, exhortations to holy living, and warnings against false teachers. The Epistles of John (1, 2, and 3 John), attributed to the apostle John, focus on the themes of love, truth, and fellowship within the Christian community. The Epistle of Jude, written by Jude, the brother of James, warns against false teachers and calls believers to contend for the faith.

The book of Revelation, authored by John, the apostle, while exiled on the island of Patmos, around 95-96 AD, is a prophetic and apocalyptic text. Revelation offers a series of visions depicting the ultimate triumph of God over evil, the final judgment, and the establishment of the new heaven and new earth. The vivid imagery and symbolism in Revelation provide hope and encouragement to persecuted Christians, affirming that Jesus Christ is the victorious King and that God's sovereign plan will prevail.

The process of compiling the New Testament books into a canonical collection involved careful discernment by early church leaders. The criteria for canonicity included apostolic authorship or association, consistency with apostolic teaching, widespread acceptance and use in the early church, and inspiration by the Holy Spirit. The writings that met these criteria were recognized as authoritative and inspired, forming the canon of the New Testament.

The early church fathers played a significant role in the canonization process. By the end of the 2nd century, church leaders such as Irenaeus, Tertullian, and Clement of Alexandria acknowledged the authority of the four Gospels, the Pauline Epistles, and other apostolic writings. Lists of accepted books, such as the Muratorian Canon (c. 170 AD), began to emerge, reflecting the growing consensus on the New Testament canon.

The Council of Carthage in 397 AD formally affirmed the 27 books of the New Testament as canonical, although the recognition of these books as authoritative scripture was already well-established in the life and practice of the church. This council, along with earlier regional councils and synods, ratified the existing consensus among the churches regarding the New Testament writings.

The transmission of the New Testament texts involved meticulous copying and preservation by scribes and scholars. The earliest manuscripts, such as papyrus fragments and codices, date back to the 2nd and 3rd centuries. Over time, the text of the New Testament was translated into various languages, including Latin, Syriac, Coptic, and eventually into vernacular languages, ensuring its accessibility to Christians across different cultures and regions.

The theological richness and doctrinal clarity of the New Testament writings have profoundly shaped Christian belief and practice throughout history. The Gospels provide the foundational narrative of Jesus' life and ministry, highlighting His teachings, miracles, and redemptive work. The Acts of the Apostles chronicles the dynamic growth of the early church and the spread of the gospel, emphasizing the role of the Holy Spirit in guiding and empowering believers.

The Pauline Epistles articulate key theological doctrines, such as justification by faith, the nature of the church, and the transformative power of the gospel. Paul's letters address specific issues within early Christian communities, offering timeless principles for living out the Christian faith. The General Epistles provide practical guidance for Christian conduct, emphasizing themes such as perseverance, love, and sound doctrine.

The book of Revelation offers a prophetic vision of God's ultimate victory over evil and the establishment of His eternal kingdom. Its apocalyptic imagery and eschatological themes provide hope and assurance to believers, affirming that God's sovereign plan will be fulfilled.

The process of writing and compiling the books of the New Testament reflects the early church's commitment to preserving and transmitting the teachings of Jesus and the apostles. The inspired nature of these writings and their authoritative status within the Christian community have ensured their enduring significance and impact. The New Testament continues to be a vital source of spiritual guidance, theological insight, and encouragement for Christians around the world, pointing believers to the person and work of Jesus Christ and the hope of eternal life in Him.

The New Testament's formation involved a complex interplay of divine inspiration, apostolic authority, and communal discernment. The writings of the New Testament emerged from the lived experiences of the early Christian community, addressing their theological, pastoral, and eschatological concerns. The careful compilation and preservation of these texts by the early church ensured that the message of Jesus Christ and the teachings of the apostles would be faithfully transmitted to future generations. The New Testament remains a testament to the enduring power of God's Word and the transformative impact of the gospel in the lives of believers.

Canonical Criteria

The formation of the New Testament canon was a process deeply rooted in the early Christian community's need to preserve and transmit the apostolic teachings faithfully. Several criteria guided the early Christians in determining which writings were to be included in the canon. These criteria ensured that the texts were authentically apostolic, theologically sound, widely accepted, and spiritually edifying.

One of the primary criteria was apostolic authorship or association. Early Christians placed a high value on writings that were believed to have been penned by the apostles themselves or their close associates. The apostles were considered the authoritative witnesses to Jesus Christ's life, death, and resurrection, and their writings were viewed as divinely inspired. For instance, the Gospels of Matthew and John were attributed to the apostles of the same names, while Mark and Luke were seen as companions of Peter and Paul, respectively.

The criterion of orthodoxy was also crucial. Writings that were consistent with the established apostolic teaching and the "rule of faith" were deemed suitable for inclusion. This meant that the texts had to align with the core doctrines that had been handed down through the apostolic tradition, such as the divinity of Christ, the Trinity, and the resurrection. Any writings that deviated from these fundamental beliefs or introduced heretical ideas were rejected.

Another significant criterion was the widespread usage and acceptance of the texts within the early Christian communities. A book that was widely read and used in liturgical settings across different congregations was more likely to be considered canonical. This widespread acceptance served as a testament to the text's authenticity and its spiritual value to the Christian community. For example, the letters of Paul were circulated among the churches and frequently cited by early church leaders, contributing to their canonical status.

The criterion of inspiration was also paramount. Early Christians believed that the Holy Spirit had inspired certain texts to communicate God's revelation. This inspiration was discerned through the text's ability to edify the church, provide sound doctrine, and convey the presence and work of the Holy Spirit. Writings that exhibited these qualities were considered to bear the marks of divine inspiration and were therefore included in the canon.

The process of canonization was not without its debates and controversies. One of the key controversies surrounded the inclusion of certain books that had varying levels of acceptance among different Christian communities. For example, the book of Revelation faced significant scrutiny and debate. While it was widely accepted in the Eastern church, the Western church was more hesitant due to its complex symbolism and apocalyptic content. Church leaders such as Athanasius of Alexandria championed its inclusion, recognizing its prophetic significance and theological depth.

The inclusion of the Epistle to the Hebrews also sparked debate. The anonymity of its authorship and its sophisticated theological arguments led some to question its apostolic origins. However, its profound Christological themes and widespread use in the Eastern church eventually secured its place in the canon. The church fathers, including Clement of Alexandria and Origen, regarded it as Pauline in theology, even if not directly written by Paul.

The status of the General Epistles (James, 2 Peter, 2 and 3 John, and Jude) also prompted discussions. These letters were sometimes questioned due to their limited circulation and doubts about their apostolic authorship. The Epistle of James, for instance, faced scrutiny over its perceived emphasis on works in relation to faith. Martin Luther famously called it an "epistle of straw" because he believed it conflicted with Paul's teachings on justification by faith alone. However, the epistle's practical wisdom and ethical instructions eventually garnered broader acceptance.

Marcion of Sinope, a 2nd-century theologian, posed one of the most significant challenges to the canonization process. Marcion proposed a truncated canon that excluded the Old Testament and accepted only a modified version of Luke's Gospel and ten Pauline epistles, rejecting what he saw as Jewish influences. His radical views forced the early church to more clearly define the canon, affirming the continuity of the Old and New Testaments and the inclusiveness of the broader collection of apostolic writings.

The Gnostic texts, which offered alternative Christian narratives and doctrines, also influenced the formation of the canon. Texts like the Gospel of Thomas and the Gospel of Mary presented teachings that were often at odds with orthodox Christian beliefs, emphasizing esoteric knowledge and spiritual elitism. The early church rejected these texts, reaffirming the necessity of writings that conformed to apostolic doctrine and were accessible to all believers.

The process of canonization involved various church councils and synods that convened to discuss and affirm the accepted books. The Synod of Hippo in 393 AD and the Councils of Carthage in 397 and 419 AD played pivotal roles in solidifying the New Testament canon. These councils ratified the 27 books that had gained widespread recognition and usage in the Christian community. The decisions of these councils were not arbitrary but reflected the consensus that had been building over the centuries regarding the authenticity and authority of these writings.

The early church fathers, such as Irenaeus, Tertullian, and Origen, significantly influenced the canonization process through their writings and theological reflections. Irenaeus, in his work "Against Heresies," emphasized the importance of the fourfold Gospel, arguing that the diversity of the four Gospels provided a complete and harmonious witness to Jesus Christ. Tertullian's writings defended the apostolic origin of the New Testament books and their doctrinal integrity. Origen's extensive biblical scholarship and his compilation of the Hexapla, a critical edition of the Old Testament, underscored the need for a reliable and authoritative New Testament canon.

The development of the codex, an early form of the book, also facilitated the canonization process. Unlike scrolls, codices could contain multiple writings in one volume, making it easier for early Christians to collect and circulate the New Testament texts. The codex format promoted the unity and coherence of the

Christian scriptures, supporting the recognition of a fixed canon.

In addition to theological and practical considerations, the early church's experience of persecution and martyrdom influenced the canonization process. The writings that provided strength, encouragement, and hope to believers facing persecution were highly valued. The New Testament books offered a theological framework for understanding suffering, perseverance, and the ultimate victory of Christ, reinforcing their significance and authority within the Christian community.

The role of the Holy Spirit in guiding the canonization process cannot be overstated. Early Christians believed that the same Spirit who inspired the apostles to write the New Testament also guided the church in recognizing and affirming these writings as canonical. This belief in the Spirit's ongoing work ensured that the canon was not merely a human construct but a divinely orchestrated collection of sacred texts.

The theological and ecclesiastical implications of the New Testament canon were profound. The canon provided a definitive body of authoritative scripture that shaped Christian doctrine, worship, and practice. It established a common foundation for teaching, preaching, and defending the faith against heresies and false teachings. The New Testament canon also fostered unity among diverse Christian communities, providing a shared source of divine revelation and guidance.

The canonization of the New Testament was a dynamic and multifaceted process, reflecting the early church's dedication to preserving the apostolic witness and discerning the authentic voice of God in the writings. The criteria of apostolic authorship, orthodoxy, widespread acceptance, and inspiration ensured that the canon was both faithful to the apostolic tradition and relevant to the spiritual needs of the church. The debates and controversies surrounding the formation of the canon highlight the rigorous and discerning approach of the early Christians, guided by the Holy Spirit, in establishing the definitive collection of New Testament scriptures.

The process of determining the New Testament canon was marked by careful discernment, theological reflection, and ecclesiastical consensus. The criteria used by early Christians ensured that the canon was authentically apostolic, theologically sound, widely accepted, and spiritually edifying. The key debates and controversies surrounding the canonization process, including the status of certain books and the challenge of heretical texts, underscore the complexity and significance of this endeavor. The New Testament canon, as recognized by the early church, continues to be the foundational text for Christian faith and practice, bearing witness to the enduring power and truth of the gospel of Jesus Christ.

Chapter 6

Comparative Analysis of the Septuagint and the Greek New Testament

Linguistic and Stylistic Features

The Septuagint and the Greek New Testament are two significant bodies of literature in early Christianity, both written in Greek but differing in linguistic and stylistic features due to their origins, purposes, and historical contexts. Understanding these differences provides valuable insights into their respective roles in conveying theological messages and shaping the early Christian faith.

The Septuagint, commonly abbreviated as LXX, is the ancient Greek translation of the Hebrew Scriptures, completed by Jewish scholars in the 3rd to 2nd centuries BCE. It was translated primarily in Alexandria, a prominent center of Hellenistic culture and learning. The primary purpose of the Septuagint was to make the Hebrew Scriptures accessible to Greek-speaking Jews who no longer spoke Hebrew fluently. As a translation, the Septuagint sought to maintain fidelity to the original Hebrew text while making it comprehensible in Greek. This often resulted in a more literal translation, reflecting Hebrew idioms and structures within the Greek language. Consequently, the Greek of the Septuagint can appear somewhat awkward or foreign to native Greek speakers, as it retains the syntactical and grammatical peculiarities of Hebrew.

In contrast, the Greek New Testament was originally composed in Greek by various authors in the 1st century AD. The New Testament texts, including the Gospels, Acts, Epistles, and Revelation, were written to address the theological, pastoral, and evangelistic needs of the early Christian communities spread throughout the Greco-Roman world. The authors of the New Testament were primarily Jewish Christians who were fluent in Greek, and they wrote in a style that was accessible to their contemporary audience. The Greek of the New Testament is characterized by its use of Koine Greek, the common dialect of the Eastern Mediterranean during this period. Koine Greek was the lingua franca of the time, used for everyday communication, commerce, and literature. This made the New Testament writings more immediately understandable to a broad audience, both Jews and Gentiles.

Linguistically speaking, the Septuagint's Greek often exhibits Semitic influences, such as the use of Hebraisms and Aramaisms, which reflect its Hebrew source material. For instance, the Septuagint frequently employs the Greek conjunction "καὶ" (kai) in a manner similar to the Hebrew "ו" (vav), often resulting in a string of clauses connected by "and." This feature can give the Septuagint a somewhat repetitive and paratactic style, as seen in Genesis 1:1-3, where each verse begins with "καὶ." Additionally, the Septuagint occasionally uses Greek words that were not commonly used in classical literature but were chosen for their ability to convey specific Hebrew concepts. For example, the word "δίκαιος" (dikaios) is used to translate the Hebrew word "צַדִּיק" (tzaddik), meaning "righteous" or "just," highlighting the Septuagint's effort to remain true to the theological vocabulary of the Hebrew Scriptures.

The Greek New Testament, on the other hand, reflects a more idiomatic and fluid use of Koine Greek, with less direct dependence on Hebrew structures. The authors employed a variety of stylistic techniques to convey their messages effectively. For example, the Gospel of Luke and the Acts of the Apostles, both attributed to Luke, showcase a polished and sophisticated Greek style, incorporating classical rhetorical elements and a high degree of literary artistry. Luke's use of medical terminology, consistent with his profession as a physician, adds another layer of nuance to his writing. The Epistles of Paul demonstrate a different stylistic approach, characterized by complex sentence structures, rhetorical questions, and theological arguments. Paul's Greek is vivid and dynamic, reflecting his passionate engagement with the issues facing his congregations.

Another notable difference is the use of quotations from the Old Testament. The New Testament frequently cites the Septuagint, reflecting its widespread use in the early

Christian community. These quotations are often adapted to fit the context of the New Testament passages, demonstrating the authors' familiarity with the Septuagint and their interpretive flexibility. For example, in Matthew 1:23, the prophecy from Isaiah 7:14 is quoted as "'Ιδοὺ ἡ παρθένος ἐν γαστρὶ ἕξει" ("Behold, the virgin shall conceive"), following the Septuagint's rendering rather than the Hebrew text, which uses the term "עלמה" (almah) meaning "young woman." This choice highlights the theological significance the New Testament writers found in the Greek version of the Scriptures.

The vocabulary and grammar of the Septuagint and the New Testament also reflect their distinct contexts. The Septuagint contains numerous Greek terms that were specifically chosen to convey Hebrew theological concepts, sometimes resulting in the creation of new semantic fields within Greek. For instance, the use of "λόγος" (logos) in the Septuagint to translate the Hebrew "דָּבָר" (dabar) meaning "word" or "thing" laid the groundwork for the profound theological significance it would later assume in the New Testament, particularly in the prologue of the Gospel of John ("Ἐν ἀρχῇ ἦν ὁ λόγος" - "In the beginning was the Word").

The New Testament, while building on this foundation, employs Greek in a manner that resonates more with the linguistic norms of its Hellenistic audience. The authors of the New Testament skillfully adapted their Greek to various genres and purposes. The Synoptic

Gospels (Matthew, Mark, and Luke) use a straightforward narrative style to recount the life and teachings of Jesus, making them accessible to a wide audience. The Gospel of John, however, employs a more poetic and symbolic style, with a strong emphasis on theological reflection and the identity of Jesus as the incarnate Word.

The epistolary literature of the New Testament, particularly the Pauline Epistles, showcases a different stylistic approach. Paul's letters are rich in rhetorical devices, such as diatribe, chiasmus, and parallelism, reflecting his training in Jewish and Greco-Roman rhetoric. His use of antithesis and contrasts, as seen in passages like Romans 5:18-19, where he contrasts Adam and Christ, demonstrates his ability to convey complex theological ideas in a compelling and memorable way.

The book of Revelation presents yet another distinct style within the New Testament. Written in an apocalyptic genre, Revelation employs vivid imagery, symbolic language, and numerology to convey its eschatological visions. The Greek of Revelation is unique, with a notable use of Hebraic syntax and grammar, reflecting its deep roots in the Jewish apocalyptic tradition. For instance, Revelation frequently uses the conjunction "καὶ" (and) to string together a series of visions, reminiscent of the paratactic style of the Septuagint.

In terms of syntax, the Septuagint often mirrors Hebrew sentence structures, which can result in less fluid Greek. This includes the frequent use of parataxis, where clauses are linked by simple conjunctions rather than complex sentences. The New Testament writers, while also using parataxis, often employ more varied and sophisticated syntactical structures. For example, Paul's use of periodic sentences, where the main clause is postponed to create suspense or emphasis, demonstrates a more advanced command of Greek rhetoric.

The stylistic features of the Septuagint and the Greek New Testament also reflect their respective theological emphases. The Septuagint, as a translation of the Hebrew Scriptures, retains a strong focus on the covenantal relationship between God and Israel, the Law, and the prophetic tradition. Its language often reflects the solemnity and sacredness of these themes. The New Testament, while rooted in the Jewish tradition, expands its theological focus to include the life, death, and resurrection of Jesus Christ, the establishment of the Church, and the new covenant. The language of the New Testament is thus imbued with a sense of urgency, proclamation, and pastoral care, reflecting its mission to spread the gospel and nurture the faith of early Christians.

Despite these differences, the Septuagint and the Greek New Testament share a common linguistic heritage that facilitated the transmission of biblical traditions from the

Jewish to the Christian communities. The Septuagint's translation choices and theological vocabulary provided a linguistic bridge that enabled the early Christians to articulate their faith in the context of Hellenistic culture. The New Testament writers, by drawing on the Septuagint and adapting its language to their own contexts, were able to communicate the gospel message in a way that was both faithful to the Jewish tradition and relevant to the Greco-Roman world.

The linguistic and stylistic features of the Septuagint and the Greek New Testament reflect their distinct origins, purposes, and contexts. The Septuagint, as a translation of the Hebrew Scriptures, retains many Hebraic features and serves as a vital link between the Hebrew and Greek-speaking Jewish communities. The Greek New Testament, composed in Koine Greek, employs a more idiomatic and fluid style suited to its diverse audiences and theological messages. Both bodies of literature, despite their differences, contribute to the rich tapestry of early Christian scripture and theology, embodying the dynamic interplay between language, culture, and divine revelation.

Shared Themes and Concepts

The Septuagint and the Greek New Testament share numerous themes and concepts that reflect their interconnectedness and the theological continuity between the Jewish Scriptures and early Christian writings. These shared themes include covenant, messianic expectations, law, wisdom, and eschatology. Understanding these commonalities and differences is essential for interpreting biblical texts and comprehending the development of early Christian theology.

One of the central themes shared between the Septuagint and the Greek New Testament is the concept of the covenant. The Septuagint frequently refers to the covenant (διαθήκη) that God established with His people, beginning with Abraham and continuing through Moses and David. This covenantal framework is foundational to the identity of Israel as God's chosen people. In Genesis 17:7, God promises to establish an everlasting covenant with Abraham and his descendants, a theme reiterated throughout the Pentateuch, Prophets, and Writings.

The New Testament builds on this covenantal theme, emphasizing the new covenant inaugurated by Jesus Christ. In the Synoptic Gospels, Jesus speaks of His blood as the blood of the new covenant (Matthew 26:28, Mark 14:24, Luke 22:20), echoing the language of the Septuagint while introducing a transformative element. The Epistle to the Hebrews elaborates on this theme, contrasting the old covenant mediated by Moses with the superior new covenant mediated by Christ (Hebrews 8:6-13). This continuity and transformation underscore the theological significance of the covenant in both texts, highlighting the fulfillment of God's promises through Jesus.

Messianic expectations also represent a significant shared theme. The Septuagint contains numerous prophecies and passages that point to a future anointed one, the Messiah, who will bring salvation and establish God's kingdom. Passages such as Isaiah 9:6-7 and Isaiah 53 in the Septuagint are interpreted messianically, with the latter describing the suffering servant whose afflictions bring healing to others. These prophecies are foundational for the development of messianic hope within Judaism.

The New Testament authors frequently cite and allude to these Septuagint passages to affirm Jesus as the long-awaited Messiah. The Gospel of Matthew, for example, repeatedly quotes the Septuagint to demonstrate that Jesus fulfills messianic prophecies, including the virgin birth (Isaiah 7:14), the flight to Egypt (Hosea 11:1), and the suffering servant (Isaiah 53). In Luke 4:18-21, Jesus reads from Isaiah 61 in the synagogue, declaring that He fulfills this prophetic mission. The New Testament thus appropriates the messianic themes of the Septuagint to present Jesus as the culmination of Israel's hopes.

The law, or Torah, is another prominent theme in both the Septuagint and the Greek New Testament. The Septuagint's translation of the Pentateuch provides the foundational legal and ethical instructions for the Jewish people. These laws encompass moral, ceremonial, and civil regulations, shaping the religious and social life of Israel. The Decalogue (Exodus 20:1-17) and the Holiness Code (Leviticus 17-26) exemplify the comprehensive nature of the Torah.

In the New Testament, the law is both upheld and reinterpreted through the lens of Christ's teachings. Jesus affirms the importance of the law, stating that He has come not to abolish it but to fulfill it (Matthew 5:17-20). The Sermon on the Mount (Matthew 5-7) offers a profound reinterpretation of the law, emphasizing the spirit rather than the letter of the commandments. Paul's epistles, particularly Romans and Galatians, explore the relationship between the law and the new covenant, arguing that believers are justified by faith in Christ rather than by works of the law (Galatians 2:16). This nuanced understanding of the law reflects both continuity with and transformation of the Septuagint's legal traditions.

Wisdom literature is another area of thematic overlap. The Septuagint includes books such as Proverbs, Ecclesiastes, and the Wisdom of Solomon, which offer reflections on wisdom, righteousness, and the fear of the Lord. Proverbs, for example, extols wisdom as the principal thing and provides practical advice for living a life pleasing to God (Proverbs 1:1-7, 4:7).

The New Testament incorporates and builds upon this wisdom tradition. Jesus is often portrayed as a teacher of divine wisdom, imparting parables and sayings that reflect the wisdom literature of the Septuagint. In Matthew 11:28-30, Jesus invites the weary to take His yoke upon them and learn from Him, emphasizing His role as a wise and gentle teacher. The Epistle of James, with its emphasis on practical wisdom, echoes the style and themes of Proverbs, urging believers to seek wisdom from above (James 1:5, 3:13-18).

Eschatology, or the study of last things, is a pervasive theme in both texts. The Septuagint contains apocalyptic visions, particularly in the books of Daniel and Isaiah, which describe the ultimate triumph of God's kingdom and the establishment of justice and peace. Daniel 7:13-14, for instance, envisions the coming of the Son of Man who will receive dominion and glory, a passage that profoundly influences New Testament eschatology.

The New Testament eschatology centers on the return of Christ and the consummation of God's kingdom. The Gospels, particularly the Olivet Discourse (Matthew 24, Mark 13, Luke 21), outline signs of the end times and the coming of the Son of Man. Paul's letters, especially 1 Thessalonians and 1 Corinthians, provide detailed teachings on the resurrection, the second coming of Christ, and the final judgment. The book of Revelation, with its vivid apocalyptic imagery, draws heavily on the eschatological themes of the Septuagint, presenting a vision of the ultimate victory of Christ and the new heaven and new earth (Revelation 21-22).

These shared themes and concepts significantly impact the interpretation of biblical texts. The Septuagint's translation choices and theological emphases provide a framework for understanding the New Testament's use of the Hebrew Scriptures. For instance, the Septuagint's rendering of Isaiah 7:14 as "a virgin shall conceive" (παρθένος) directly influences Matthew's citation of this prophecy in relation to the birth of Jesus. This translation shapes the Christological interpretation of the passage, underscoring the theological continuity between the Old and New Testaments.

Furthermore, the differences in linguistic and stylistic features between the Septuagint and the Greek New Testament reflect the evolving contexts and audiences of these texts. The Septuagint's more literal translation style can preserve Hebrew idioms and concepts that might otherwise be lost in translation, providing a rich source for understanding Jewish thought and practice. The New Testament's more idiomatic Greek, on the other hand, demonstrates the adaptability of the Christian message to a broader Hellenistic audience, making the gospel accessible and relevant to diverse cultural contexts.

The theological implications of these similarities and differences are profound. The shared themes of covenant, messianic expectation, law, wisdom, and eschatology reveal a deep continuity in the divine narrative, while the distinct approaches to these themes highlight the transformative impact of Christ's incarnation, death, and resurrection. This duality of continuity and transformation enriches the theological discourse, enabling a fuller appreciation of the unified yet diverse witness of Scripture.

Moreover, the interplay between the Septuagint and the Greek New Testament underscores the importance of intertextuality in biblical interpretation. Understanding how the New Testament writers engaged with and reinterpreted the Septuagint can illuminate their theological intentions and the message they sought to convey. For example, Paul's use of Abraham's faith in Romans 4, drawing from Genesis 15:6 in the Septuagint, illustrates his argument for justification by faith apart from works of the law. This intertextual approach provides a deeper insight into Paul's theological reasoning and his continuity with the Abrahamic covenant.

The shared themes and concepts between the Septuagint and the Greek New Testament demonstrate the interconnectedness of the Jewish and Christian Scriptures, reflecting a unified divine narrative that spans both Testaments. The linguistic and stylistic differences between the texts, shaped by their distinct contexts and purposes, enhance our understanding of their theological messages and their relevance to diverse audiences. The impact of these similarities and differences on biblical interpretation is profound, offering rich insights into the continuity and transformation inherent in the biblical witness to God's redemptive work in history. By exploring these themes and their intertextual relationships, we gain a deeper appreciation of the theological depth and coherence of the Scriptures, fostering a more nuanced and informed engagement with the biblical text.

Chapter 7

The Role of the Septuagint in the Early Church

Patristic Writings and Exegesis

The Septuagint played a pivotal role in the patristic writings and exegesis of the early Church Fathers, serving as a bridge between the Hebrew Scriptures and Christian theology. The early Christian writers, many of whom were well-versed in Greek, relied heavily on the Septuagint for their scriptural references and theological reflections. This reliance on the Septuagint not only shaped their understanding of the Old Testament but also influenced the development of Christian doctrine and exegesis.

The early Church Fathers, including figures such as Justin Martyr, Irenaeus, Clement of Alexandria, Origen, and Augustine, frequently cited the Septuagint in their apologetic and exegetical works. These patristic authors viewed the Septuagint as an authoritative text that conveyed divine revelation to both Jews and Gentiles. For them, the Septuagint was not merely a translation of the Hebrew Scriptures but a divinely inspired version that held significant theological value.

Justin Martyr, one of the earliest apologists, utilized the Septuagint extensively in his dialogues with Jewish interlocutors. In his work "Dialogue with Trypho," Justin argues that the prophecies in the Septuagint, such as Isaiah 7:14 and Isaiah 53, find their fulfillment in Jesus Christ. Justin emphasizes the Septuagint's prophetic accuracy and its role in revealing Christ as the Messiah. He contends that the translation process itself was guided by the Holy Spirit, thus lending the Septuagint an authority comparable to the original Hebrew text.

Irenaeus, in his seminal work "Against Heresies," also relies heavily on the Septuagint to refute Gnostic interpretations of Scripture and to affirm the continuity between the Old and New Testaments. Irenaeus highlights the consistency of God's salvific plan as revealed in the Septuagint and fulfilled in Christ. He frequently quotes passages from the Septuagint to demonstrate the unity of Scripture and to counter heretical teachings that sought to undermine the authority of the Old Testament.

Clement of Alexandria and Origen, prominent theologians and exegetes, further developed the use of the Septuagint in their scholarly works. Clement's writings, such as "Stromata" and "Paedagogus," integrate philosophical and scriptural exegesis, drawing from the Septuagint to elucidate Christian doctrine and ethics. Clement sees the Septuagint as a critical link in the pedagogical process by which God educates humanity, leading them from the elementary teachings of the Old Testament to the fullness of revelation in Christ.

Origen's contributions to biblical scholarship and exegesis are particularly noteworthy. His work "Hexapla" was a monumental effort to compare various versions of the Old Testament, including the Hebrew text, the Septuagint, and other Greek translations. Origen's meticulous study of the Septuagint aimed to clarify textual variants and to enhance the accuracy of scriptural interpretation. He regarded the Septuagint as essential for understanding the theological depth of the Old Testament and its Christological fulfillment. In his commentaries, Origen often employed allegorical and typological methods, using the Septuagint to uncover deeper spiritual meanings and to connect Old Testament narratives with New Testament realities.

Augustine, one of the most influential Church Fathers, also affirmed the importance of the Septuagint. In his works, such as "City of God" and "Confessions," Augustine defends the Septuagint's authority and its role in the Christian canon. He argues that the Septuagint was providentially used by God to prepare the Gentile world for the gospel. Augustine acknowledges the Septuagint's divergences from the Hebrew text but views these variations as divinely intended to reveal different facets of God's truth. His writings reflect a deep appreciation for the theological richness of the Septuagint and its contribution to Christian doctrine.

The patristic exegesis of the Septuagint was not limited to doctrinal and apologetic purposes; it also played a significant role in liturgical and devotional practices. The Psalms, as rendered in the Septuagint, were central to the prayer life and worship of the early Church. Church Fathers like Athanasius and John Chrysostom wrote extensive commentaries on the Psalms, drawing from the Septuagint's text to offer spiritual insights and pastoral guidance. The use of the Septuagint Psalms in liturgy and private devotion underscored their importance in the spiritual formation of early Christians.

Moreover, the Septuagint's influence extended to the development of Christian typology and allegory. The Church Fathers often interpreted Old Testament events, persons, and institutions as prefigurations of Christ and His Church. For instance, the account of the Passover lamb in Exodus, as translated in the Septuagint, was seen as a type of Christ, the Lamb of God who takes away the sin of the world. The crossing of the Red Sea was viewed as a prefigurement of baptism, and the manna in the wilderness as a foreshadowing of the Eucharist. These typological interpretations, grounded in the Septuagint, enriched the theological and sacramental understanding of early Christianity.

The Septuagint also provided a framework for understanding the moral and ethical teachings of the Old Testament. The Church Fathers, particularly in their homilies and catechetical instructions, used the ethical exhortations found in the Septuagint to guide the conduct of Christian believers. They emphasized virtues such as humility, charity, and obedience, drawing on examples from the lives of Old Testament saints. The wisdom literature of the Septuagint, especially the books of Proverbs, Ecclesiastes, and the Wisdom of Solomon, offered practical guidance for living a righteous life in accordance with God's will.

In addition to its role in exegesis and theology, the Septuagint influenced the formation of the Christian canon. The early Church's acceptance of the Septuagint as Scripture contributed to the inclusion of certain books, such as the Deuterocanonical books, in the Christian Old Testament. These books, which were part of the Septuagint but not the Hebrew canon, were regarded by many Church Fathers as inspired and authoritative. This acceptance reflected the broader Hellenistic context in which the early Church emerged and the recognition of the Septuagint's significance in conveying God's revelation to the Gentile world.

The use of the Septuagint in patristic writings also facilitated the engagement with Hellenistic philosophy and culture. The Church Fathers, particularly those of the Alexandrian school, employed the language and concepts of Greek philosophy to articulate and defend Christian doctrine. They used the Septuagint's rendering of key theological terms, such as "logos" (word) and "sophia" (wisdom), to communicate the truths of the Christian faith in a manner that was intelligible and compelling to their Greek-speaking contemporaries.

This synthesis of biblical exegesis and philosophical reflection enriched the intellectual and spiritual life of the early Church.

The influence of the Septuagint on patristic exegesis is evident in the theological controversies and doctrinal formulations of the early Church. Debates over the nature of Christ, the Trinity, and salvation often hinged on scriptural interpretation, with the Septuagint providing crucial texts for these discussions. For example, the Arian controversy, which revolved around the divinity of Christ, involved extensive exegesis of passages like Proverbs 8:22-31, where the Septuagint's rendering of "The Lord created me" was central to the debate. The Nicene Fathers, including Athanasius, argued for the consubstantiality of the Son with the Father, using the Septuagint's text to support their doctrinal positions.

The Septuagint was integral to the patristic writings and exegesis of the early Church Fathers. It served as a foundational text for theological reflection, doctrinal formulation, and scriptural interpretation. The Church Fathers' reliance on the Septuagint underscored its authority and significance within early Christianity, shaping the development of Christian doctrine and the spiritual life of the Church. Through their engagement with the Septuagint, the Church Fathers articulated a vision of Scripture that bridged the Jewish and Hellenistic worlds, affirming the continuity of God's revelation and its fulfillment in Christ. The Septuagint's influence on patristic exegesis continues to resonate in

Christian theology and biblical interpretation, highlighting the enduring legacy of this ancient translation

Liturgical Use

The Septuagint, as the Greek translation of the Hebrew Scriptures, held a central role in early Christian liturgical practices and theological development. Its influence permeated various aspects of worship, from readings and hymns to prayers and doctrinal teachings, shaping the spiritual and intellectual life of the early Church. The Septuagint's significance in liturgical settings and theological discourse highlights its foundational place in the nascent Christian community.

In early Christian liturgy, the Septuagint was the primary scriptural text. The Greek-speaking Christians of the early Church, spread across the Hellenistic world, naturally adopted the Septuagint as their Bible. This translation provided a common scriptural foundation that could be readily understood by Greek-speaking believers, facilitating the inclusion of Scripture in communal worship. The public reading of the Scriptures, a practice inherited from Jewish synagogue worship, was central to Christian liturgical gatherings. The Septuagint was read aloud during these assemblies, offering the faithful a direct encounter with the word of God.

The Psalms, as rendered in the Septuagint, played a particularly prominent role in early Christian worship. These ancient hymns and prayers were integral to the liturgical life of the Church, recited or sung during various services. The Psalms expressed a range of human emotions and spiritual experiences, resonating deeply with the early Christian community. Church Fathers like Athanasius and John Chrysostom wrote commentaries on the Psalms, emphasizing their importance in both private devotion and communal worship. The Septuagint's translation of the Psalms became the basis for the Christian practice of chanting and singing these sacred texts, a tradition that continues in various Christian liturgical traditions today.

The use of the Septuagint in early Christian worship extended beyond the Psalms. Other Old Testament books, including the Prophets and the Pentateuch, were also read and expounded upon in liturgical settings. The lectionary system, which organized the reading of Scripture over the course of the liturgical year, often drew from the Septuagint. This practice ensured that the faithful were exposed to a comprehensive selection of scriptural passages, grounding their faith and worship in the breadth of God's revelation.

The Septuagint's theological significance for the early Church was profound. It provided a textual basis for the articulation of Christian doctrine and the defense of the faith against various heresies. The early Church Fathers, many of whom were fluent in Greek and well-versed in the Septuagint, used this translation to develop and communicate key theological concepts. The Septuagint's rendering of certain Hebrew terms and passages often informed their understanding of important doctrinal issues.

One of the central theological developments influenced by the Septuagint was the doctrine of the Trinity. The Septuagint's translation of passages like Genesis 1:26, where God says, "Let us make man in our image," and Isaiah 6:8, where God asks, "Whom shall I send, and who will go for us?" provided a scriptural foundation for the early Christian understanding of the triune nature of God. The use of plural pronouns in these passages suggested a multiplicity within the Godhead, which early theologians interpreted as an indication of the Trinity.

The doctrine of the incarnation was also deeply rooted in the Septuagint. Prophecies such as Isaiah 7:14, which the Septuagint renders as "Behold, a virgin shall conceive and bear a son," were seen as foretelling the birth of Jesus Christ. The Gospel of Matthew explicitly cites this passage to demonstrate the fulfillment of this prophecy in the virgin birth of Jesus (Matthew 1:23). The Septuagint's translation choice, using the Greek word "parthenos" (virgin), played a crucial role in shaping the early Church's Christological beliefs.

The Septuagint was instrumental in the development of soteriology, the doctrine of salvation. The sacrificial system described in the Septuagint's translation of

Leviticus, with its emphasis on atonement and purification, provided a typological framework for understanding Christ's sacrificial death. Passages such as Isaiah 53, which describe the suffering servant who bears the sins of many, were interpreted as prophetic foreshadowings of Christ's atoning work. The New Testament writers, particularly in the Epistle to the Hebrews, draw heavily on the Septuagint's language to explain how Christ's death fulfills and surpasses the sacrificial system of the Old Covenant.

The Septuagint's influence extended to ecclesiology, the doctrine of the Church. The early Christians saw themselves as the new Israel, the continuation and fulfillment of God's covenant people. Passages from the Septuagint, such as those in Isaiah and Jeremiah that speak of a new covenant and a restored people of God, were appropriated to describe the identity and mission of the Church. The language of the Septuagint helped early Christians articulate their self-understanding as the Body of Christ and the spiritual heirs of Israel's promises.

In addition to doctrinal development, the Septuagint played a role in the exegetical methods of the early Church. The Church Fathers employed various interpretative approaches, including allegorical, typological, and literal exegesis, drawing on the Septuagint to elucidate the deeper spiritual meanings of Scripture. Origen's allegorical method, for example, sought to uncover the spiritual truths hidden beneath the literal sense of the text. He used the Septuagint to illustrate how Old Testament events and figures prefigured Christ and the Church, revealing a coherent divine plan throughout salvation history.

The typological interpretation, championed by figures like Irenaeus and Augustine, saw the events and institutions of the Old Testament as foreshadows of New Testament realities. The Septuagint's portrayal of figures like Adam, Moses, and David provided rich typological material that the Church Fathers used to draw connections between the Old and New Testaments. Adam was seen as a type of Christ, with Christ being the new Adam who brings life where the first Adam brought death. Moses, the lawgiver and deliverer, prefigured Christ as the ultimate lawgiver and redeemer. David, the shepherd-king, pointed to Christ as the Good Shepherd and the King of kings.

The literal-historical method, also employed by the Church Fathers, involved a careful reading of the Septuagint's text to understand its original context and meaning. This approach sought to preserve the historical integrity of the Old Testament narratives while recognizing their significance for Christian faith and practice. The Septuagint's translation choices and interpretative nuances provided valuable insights into the historical and cultural context of the biblical events, enriching the early Church's understanding of God's dealings with His people.

The Septuagint also had a significant impact on the formation of the Christian canon. The early Church's acceptance of the Septuagint as Scripture influenced the inclusion of certain books that were part of the Septuagint but not the Hebrew canon. These books, known as the Deuterocanonical books, were valued for their theological and spiritual insights. The Septuagint's broader canon provided the early Christians with a rich repository of texts that shaped their theology and practice.

It was integral to early Christian liturgical practices and theological development. Its use in worship, doctrinal formulation, and scriptural interpretation underscores its central place in the life of the early Church. The Septuagint's translation of the Hebrew Scriptures provided a common scriptural foundation for Greek-speaking Christians, facilitating their engagement with God's word in a language they could understand. Its influence on the development of key doctrines, such as the Trinity, the incarnation, and soteriology, highlights its theological significance. The Septuagint's role in the exegetical methods of the Church Fathers, from allegorical and typological to literal-historical interpretation, demonstrates its versatility and depth. The inclusion of the Septuagint's broader canon in the Christian Scriptures enriched the theological and spiritual heritage of the early Church. The enduring legacy of the Septuagint in Christian theology and worship testifies to its profound impact on the faith and practice of the early Christian community.

Chapter 8

Textual Criticism and the Septuagint

Methods and Challenges

The scholarly discipline of analyzing and comparing ancient manuscripts to reconstruct the most accurate version of a text, plays a crucial role in the study of the Septuagint. The process involves examining various textual witnesses, including manuscripts, quotations by early writers, and ancient translations. The goal is to identify and correct errors, understand the history of the text, and provide a reliable foundation for interpretation.

The methods of textual criticism applied to the Septuagint begin with the collection and comparison of extant manuscripts. Unlike the Hebrew Bible, which has a more unified textual tradition, the Septuagint exists in a wide array of manuscripts that display significant variation. These manuscripts are divided into different textual families or recensions, each with distinct characteristics. The primary task of textual critics is to collate these manuscripts, noting variations and attempting to determine which readings are original and which are later alterations.

One of the central methods used in textual criticism of the Septuagint is the examination of external evidence, which includes the manuscripts themselves. The oldest and most significant Septuagint manuscripts include the Codex Vaticanus, Codex Sinaiticus, and Codex Alexandrinus, all dating from the 4th and 5th centuries CE. These codices provide valuable insight into the text of the Septuagint, but they also exhibit differences that reflect the complex transmission history of the text. By comparing these and other manuscripts, scholars can identify patterns of variation and assess the reliability of different textual traditions.

Another important method is internal evidence analysis, which involves evaluating the context and content of the readings. Textual critics look for readings that best explain the origin of the variants. This includes considering factors such as the linguistic and stylistic features of the text, the coherence of the passage, and the plausibility of scribal errors. For example, a more difficult or less smooth reading is often preferred, based on the principle that scribes were more likely to simplify or harmonize the text rather than make it more complex.

The process of reconstructing the original text of the Septuagint also involves the use of ancient translations and quotations by early Christian and Jewish writers. These sources can provide evidence of the Septuagint text in use before the surviving manuscripts were written. Early translations into languages such as Latin, Coptic, Syriac, and Armenian, as well as quotations by

Church Fathers and Jewish writers like Philo and Josephus, offer additional data points for textual critics. By examining these translations and quotations, scholars can trace the development of the text and identify early readings that may have been lost in later manuscript traditions.

One of the significant challenges in the textual criticism of the Septuagint is the existence of multiple recensions or revisions. Throughout its history, the Septuagint was subject to various attempts to standardize and revise the text. Notable among these are the revisions attributed to Origen, Lucian, and Hesychius in the 3rd and 4th centuries CE. Origen's Hexapla, for instance, was a monumental work that placed the Hebrew text alongside various Greek translations, including the Septuagint, in parallel columns. Origen's goal was to address discrepancies between the Septuagint and the Hebrew text, but his work also introduced new variants into the textual tradition.

The revisions by Lucian and Hesychius aimed to produce more consistent and standardized texts for use in the Church. These revisions reflect the influence of the developing Byzantine and Alexandrian text types, each with its editorial tendencies. The presence of these recensions complicates the task of textual critics, as they must distinguish between original readings and later editorial changes. Understanding the historical and geographical context of these revisions helps scholars assess their impact on the transmission of the Septuagint.

Another challenge in the textual criticism of the Septuagint is the impact of scribal practices and errors. Scribes copying the manuscripts of the Septuagint could introduce a range of errors, including omissions, additions, substitutions, and transpositions of words or phrases. Some errors were unintentional, resulting from misreading or mishearing the text, while others were intentional, aimed at harmonizing passages, clarifying meanings, or aligning the text with theological or doctrinal views. Textual critics must carefully analyze these variations to determine their origin and significance.

The diversity of the Septuagint manuscripts also reflects the broad geographical spread of the text and its use by different Jewish and Christian communities. This geographical diversity means that the Septuagint was subject to local adaptations and changes. Textual critics must consider the provenance of the manuscripts and the historical context in which they were produced. The study of regional text types, such as the Alexandrian, Western, and Byzantine, helps scholars understand how the Septuagint evolved in different areas and how these regional variations influenced the overall transmission of the text.

The discovery of new manuscripts and advances in technology continue to enhance the field of textual criticism. The Dead Sea Scrolls, for instance, include fragments of Greek translations of the Hebrew Scriptures that predate the major Septuagint codices. These scrolls provide critical evidence for the early form of the Septuagint and its use within the Jewish community. Modern techniques, such as digital imaging and computer-assisted collation, allow scholars to examine manuscripts with greater precision and to compare vast amounts of data more efficiently.

The textual criticism of the Septuagint is not only about reconstructing the original text but also about understanding the historical and cultural context of its transmission. The variations and revisions in the Septuagint manuscripts reflect the dynamic nature of the text and its adaptation to different communities and theological perspectives. By studying these variations, scholars gain insights into the development of Jewish and Christian thought and the ways in which the Scriptures were interpreted and used in different contexts.

The role of textual criticism extends beyond academic scholarship; it has practical implications for modern translations and interpretations of the Bible. A critical edition of the Septuagint, based on rigorous textual analysis, provides a reliable foundation for translators and theologians. It ensures that modern readers have access to a text that closely approximates the original writings, allowing for more accurate and meaningful engagement with the Scriptures.

Textual criticism of the Septuagint involves meticulous methods of comparing manuscripts, analyzing internal and external evidence, and understanding the historical context of the text's transmission. The challenges of multiple recensions, scribal errors, and geographical diversity complicate this task, but they also enrich our understanding of the Septuagint's history and significance. Advances in technology and the discovery of new manuscripts continue to advance the field, providing deeper insights into the Septuagint's development and its role in Jewish and Christian traditions. Through the work of textual criticism, scholars strive to reconstruct the most accurate version of the Septuagint, preserving its legacy and enhancing our appreciation of its theological and historical

Major Critical Editions

Major critical editions of the Septuagint have significantly contributed to biblical scholarship, each bringing unique insights and advancements in understanding the text's history and transmission. These critical editions aim to reconstruct the most accurate form of the Septuagint by examining the wealth of manuscript evidence, ancient translations, and patristic citations.

One of the pioneering critical editions is the "Editio Sixtina," commissioned by Pope Sixtus V and published in 1587. This edition was based on the Codex Vaticanus, one of the oldest and most important manuscripts of the Septuagint. While it was a significant achievement for its time, the Editio Sixtina had limitations due to the lack of access to other important manuscripts and the constraints of the printing technology of the era. Nevertheless, it laid the groundwork for subsequent scholarly efforts and was a foundational text for many later editions.

The Cambridge Edition of the Septuagint, also known as "The Larger Cambridge Septuagint," edited by H.B. Swete, is another monumental work in the history of Septuagint studies. Published in three volumes between 1887 and 1894, this edition utilized a broader array of manuscript evidence than the Editio Sixtina. Swete's edition included critical apparatus that detailed the variants found in different manuscripts, providing scholars with essential data for textual analysis. This edition made the Septuagint more accessible to English-speaking scholars and advanced the study of its textual history.

The Göttingen Septuagint, an ongoing project initiated by Alfred Rahlfs in the early 20th century and continued by numerous scholars, represents the most comprehensive and detailed critical edition of the Septuagint. The Göttingen edition is distinguished by its meticulous collation of all available manuscript evidence, including papyri, codices, and quotations from early Christian and Jewish literature. Each volume of the

Göttingen Septuagint focuses on a specific book or group of books, presenting a critical text along with an extensive apparatus that documents the textual variants. This edition has become the gold standard in Septuagint studies, providing the most authoritative text for scholarly research.

The critical edition of the Septuagint by Henry Barclay Swete, known as "The Old Testament in Greek According to the Septuagint," published between 1887 and 1901, made significant contributions by incorporating a wider range of manuscripts than previous editions. Swete's work included valuable introductions and appendices that provided context and analysis of the textual variants. This edition was instrumental in advancing the understanding of the Septuagint's textual history and its relationship to the Hebrew Bible.

The Oxford Septuagint, edited by Alan E. Brooke and Norman McLean, is another noteworthy critical edition. This work, although not as extensive as the Göttingen Septuagint, provided a valuable critical text and apparatus for several books of the Septuagint. The Oxford edition was particularly important for its careful consideration of the relationship between the Septuagint and the Masoretic Text, the authoritative Hebrew text of the Jewish Bible. This comparison helped scholars understand the translation techniques and theological perspectives of the Septuagint translators.

The "Rahlfs-Hanhart Septuagint," a revision of Alfred Rahlfs' earlier work, is a widely used critical edition that offers a reliable text for both academic and ecclesiastical purposes. This edition provides a critical apparatus that includes the most important textual variants, making it a valuable resource for students and scholars. The Rahlfs-Hanhart edition strikes a balance between accessibility and scholarly rigor, contributing to its widespread adoption in Septuagint studies.

The importance of textual criticism in understanding the Septuagint and its transmission cannot be overstated. Textual criticism allows scholars to reconstruct the most original form of the Septuagint, shedding light on the history of its composition and dissemination. By examining the various manuscripts and textual witnesses, scholars can trace the development of the text over time and identify the influences of different scribal traditions and theological perspectives.

One of the key contributions of textual criticism is the identification and analysis of textual variants. Variants arise from the process of copying and transmitting the text, with scribes introducing changes either intentionally or unintentionally. These changes can include omissions, additions, alterations, and harmonizations. Textual critics seek to understand the reasons behind these variants, which can reveal much about the scribes' attitudes, theological beliefs, and the historical context in which they worked.

The study of textual variants also provides insights into the relationship between the Septuagint and the Hebrew Bible. By comparing the Septuagint with the Masoretic Text and other ancient versions, scholars can identify differences in translation and interpretation. These differences can highlight the theological and exegetical tendencies of the Septuagint translators, offering a window into the religious and cultural milieu of the Hellenistic Jewish community. For example, certain renderings in the Septuagint reflect a more Hellenistic understanding of Jewish traditions, which can be contrasted with the more conservative approach of the Masoretic Text.

Textual criticism is essential for understanding the historical and geographical spread of the Septuagint. The Septuagint was used by Jewish communities throughout the Hellenistic world, and later by early Christians. The variations in the text can indicate regional differences in its transmission and usage. By studying these regional variations, scholars can map the diffusion of the Septuagint and gain insights into the dynamics of ancient Jewish and Christian communities. This geographical analysis helps to reconstruct the complex history of the text and its reception across different cultures and epochs.

The role of textual criticism extends to the theological and doctrinal developments within early Christianity. The New Testament writers frequently quoted the Septuagint, and the variations in these quotations can reveal the interpretative strategies employed by the early Christians. Textual criticism helps to identify these variations and understand their theological implications. For instance, the use of certain Septuagint readings in the New Testament can illuminate how early Christians understood and applied the Old Testament prophecies to the life and mission of Jesus Christ.

The critical editions of the Septuagint, with their detailed apparatus and scholarly analysis, provide the necessary tools for engaging in this type of textual criticism. They offer a reliable text for translation and interpretation, enabling scholars to delve deeper into the complexities of the Septuagint's transmission and its impact on religious thought. These editions are indispensable for producing accurate and informed translations of the Septuagint, which in turn influence contemporary biblical scholarship and theological reflection.

Furthermore, textual criticism contributes to the broader field of biblical studies by fostering a nuanced understanding of the development of the biblical canon. The Septuagint includes books that are not found in the Hebrew Bible, known as the Deuterocanonical books or Apocrypha. The inclusion and exclusion of these books in different canonical traditions reflect the diverse historical and theological contexts of Jewish and Christian communities. Textual criticism helps to explore these canonical differences and their implications for the development of the biblical canon.

The study of the Septuagint through textual criticism also enhances our understanding of ancient languages and linguistics. The translation techniques used by the Septuagint translators provide insights into the linguistic interplay between Hebrew and Greek. Scholars can examine how Hebrew idioms and expressions were rendered into Greek, shedding light on the translators' linguistic choices and their adaptation of the text to a Hellenistic audience. This linguistic analysis contributes to the broader study of ancient translation practices and the interaction between different linguistic and cultural traditions.

Major critical editions of the Septuagint have profoundly impacted biblical scholarship, each offering unique contributions to the understanding of the text's history and transmission. Textual criticism is indispensable for reconstr1ucting the original text, analyzing variants, and understanding the relationship between the Septuagint and the Hebrew Bible. It provides insights into the historical, geographical, and theological contexts of the Septuagint, illuminating its role in early Jewish and Christian communities. The critical editions serve as essential tools for scholars, enabling them to produce accurate translations and engage in informed theological reflection. Through textual criticism, the Septuagint's rich and complex legacy continues to be explored, enriching our comprehension of the biblical tradition and its enduring influence.

Chapter 9

Modern Translations and the Septuagint

Influence on Contemporary Bibles

The influence of the Septuagint on contemporary Bible translations is profound and multifaceted, shaping how modern readers understand the Old Testament. As one of the earliest and most significant translations of the Hebrew Scriptures, the Septuagint provides a critical bridge between the original Hebrew text and subsequent translations into various languages, including English.

The Septuagint, translated in the 3rd and 2nd centuries BCE, was the first major effort to render the Hebrew Scriptures into Greek. This translation was essential for Hellenistic Jews who were more familiar with Greek than Hebrew, and it played a significant role in spreading Jewish scriptures throughout the Greek-speaking world. The Septuagint's influence extends beyond its initial Jewish audience, impacting early Christian communities and the development of the Christian canon.

One of the key ways the Septuagint has influenced contemporary Bible translations is through its use in the New Testament. The New Testament writers frequently quoted the Septuagint rather than the Hebrew Bible. For example, Matthew's Gospel often cites the Septuagint to demonstrate how Jesus fulfills Old Testament prophecies. This reliance on the Septuagint established a precedent for its use in Christian Scripture, which in turn affects how contemporary translators approach the Old Testament.

The Septuagint's wording and interpretations are sometimes reflected in modern translations, especially when they align closely with the New Testament quotations. For instance, the prophecy in Isaiah 7:14, rendered in the Septuagint as "a virgin shall conceive and bear a son," significantly influenced the Christian interpretation of this passage as referring to the virgin birth of Jesus. This translation choice has been retained in many English versions, such as the King James Version (KJV) and the New International Version (NIV), highlighting the Septuagint's enduring impact.

The Septuagint's influence is also evident in the inclusion of the Deuterocanonical books, also known as the Apocrypha, in certain Christian traditions. These books, which are part of the Septuagint but not the Hebrew Bible, were accepted in the early Christian canon and are included in the Roman Catholic and Eastern Orthodox Bibles. Contemporary translations that include these books, such as the New Revised Standard Version (NRSV) with Apocrypha, owe their inclusion to the Septuagint's canonical status in these traditions. This inclusion enriches the theological and historical context of the Old Testament for readers who use these translations.

The Septuagint has also influenced the textual criticism and scholarly analysis underlying contemporary Bible translations. Modern translators often consult the Septuagint to understand how ancient Jewish and early Christian communities interpreted the Hebrew Scriptures. The Septuagint provides alternative readings and interpretations that can clarify ambiguous or difficult passages in the Hebrew text. For example, differences between the Hebrew Masoretic Text and the Septuagint can shed light on how certain verses were understood in antiquity and help translators choose the most appropriate rendering for contemporary readers.

Additionally, the Septuagint has contributed to the development of critical editions of the Old Testament, which form the basis for many modern translations. Scholars use the Septuagint alongside the Masoretic Text, the Dead Sea Scrolls, and other ancient witnesses to reconstruct the most accurate text possible. This process, known as textual criticism, involves comparing these sources to identify and correct errors, omissions, and alterations that may have occurred over centuries of transmission. The critical apparatus of contemporary translations, such as the Biblia Hebraica Stuttgartensia (BHS) and the Hebrew University Bible, often references the Septuagint to provide readers with a comprehensive view of the textual history and variations.

The influence of the Septuagint is also apparent in the translation philosophy of certain contemporary versions. Some translations, like the NRSV and the New American Bible (NAB), adopt a more ecumenical approach that takes into account the Septuagint's readings, especially when they differ significantly from the Masoretic Text. This approach reflects a recognition of the Septuagint's historical and theological importance and aims to present a more holistic view of the biblical text. By incorporating the Septuagint's insights, these translations offer readers a richer and more nuanced understanding of the Scriptures.

The Septuagint's impact extends to the linguistic and stylistic choices made in contemporary translations. The translators of the Septuagint employed various strategies to render the Hebrew text into Greek, sometimes choosing literal translations and other times opting for more interpretative renderings. These choices have influenced how modern translators handle similar challenges. For example, the Septuagint's translation of the Hebrew term "chesed," often rendered as "mercy" or "steadfast love," provides a precedent for how to capture the nuances of Hebrew vocabulary in another language. Contemporary translations continue to grapple with these linguistic challenges, often looking to the Septuagint for guidance.

Moreover, the Septuagint's theological interpretations and expansions have left a lasting mark on biblical exegesis and translation. The Septuagint sometimes reflects a theological agenda, interpreting the Hebrew text in ways that emphasize certain doctrinal points. These interpretations have been incorporated into the Christian theological tradition and have influenced how certain passages are understood and translated. For instance, the Septuagint's rendering of Isaiah 53, with its emphasis on the suffering servant, has shaped Christian readings of this passage as a prophecy of Jesus' passion and has influenced how it is translated in Christian Bibles.

The Septuagint also serves as a valuable resource for understanding the historical and cultural context of the biblical text. Its translation reflects the Hellenistic milieu in which it was produced, offering insights into how Jewish communities engaged with Greek language and culture. Contemporary translations that aim to be more historically informed, such as the Jewish Publication Society (JPS) Tanakh, benefit from the Septuagint's perspective on the interplay between Hebrew and Greek thought. This historical awareness enriches the translation process and helps modern readers appreciate the complex background of the biblical text.

The study of the Septuagint has led to numerous academic publications, commentaries, and research projects that explore its text, history, and impact. This body of scholarship informs contemporary translations by providing a deeper understanding of the Septuagint's role in the development of the biblical canon and its reception in Jewish and Christian traditions. The insights gained from Septuagint studies contribute to the accuracy and depth of modern Bible translations.

The Septuagint's influence also extends to the pedagogical realm, shaping how the Bible is taught and understood in educational settings. Seminary and university courses on biblical studies often include the Septuagint as a key text, highlighting its importance for understanding the Old Testament and its interpretation in the New Testament. This academic focus on the Septuagint equips future translators, theologians, and clergy with the knowledge and skills needed to engage critically with the biblical text. The Septuagint thus plays a vital role in shaping the next generation of biblical scholarship and translation.

It serves as a common ground for Jewish and Christian scholars, offering a shared textual heritage that can foster mutual understanding and respect. Contemporary translations that incorporate the Septuagint's readings, such as the NRSV and the Common English Bible (CEB), reflect a commitment to bridging historical and theological divides. By acknowledging the Septuagint's significance, these translations promote a more inclusive and dialogical approach to the Bible.

The Septuagint has profoundly influenced contemporary Bible translations through its use in the New Testament, its inclusion of the Deuterocanonical books, and its contributions to textual criticism and scholarly analysis. The Septuagint's linguistic, stylistic, and theological choices have shaped modern translation philosophies and practices, enriching the understanding of the biblical text. Its historical and cultural insights, academic scholarship, and role in interfaith dialogue continue to inform and inspire contemporary translations, ensuring that the legacy of the Septuagint endures in the ongoing study and interpretation of the Scriptures.

Translational Philosophies

Translational philosophies vary widely in their approach to the Septuagint, each aiming to balance fidelity to the original text with readability and comprehension for contemporary audiences. These philosophies range from formal equivalence, which emphasizes a word-for-word translation, to dynamic equivalence, which focuses on conveying the meaning and spirit of the text in a more accessible manner. The choice of translational philosophy significantly influences how the Septuagint is rendered in modern translations.

Formal equivalence, also known as literal translation, strives to maintain the exact words and structure of the original text. This approach is particularly favored by translations such as the New American Standard Bible (NASB) and the English Standard Version (ESV). When applied to the Septuagint, formal equivalence aims to preserve the specific Greek vocabulary and grammatical forms, providing a close approximation of the original text. This method is valuable for academic and theological study, as it allows readers to engage with the text's nuances and intricacies. However, it can sometimes result in a translation that feels archaic or stilted to modern readers.

In contrast, dynamic equivalence, or thought-for-thought translation, prioritizes conveying the underlying meaning and intent of the original text. This approach is exemplified by translations such as the New International Version (NIV) and the New Living Translation (NLT). Translators using dynamic equivalence focus on making the text understandable and relatable to contemporary audiences. When translating the Septuagint, they might choose to render idiomatic expressions and culturally specific references in a way that resonates with modern readers. While this method enhances readability and accessibility, it may occasionally lead to interpretations that deviate from the original wording.

One notable modern translation of the Septuagint is the New English Translation of the Septuagint (NETS). The NETS adopts a philosophy that combines elements of both formal and dynamic equivalence, seeking to balance accuracy with readability. It aims to present the Septuagint as it would have been understood by its original Hellenistic Jewish audience while also making it accessible to contemporary readers. The NETS provides a detailed introduction and extensive footnotes that offer insights into the translation choices and the relationship between the Septuagint and the Hebrew

Bible. This translation is particularly valuable for scholars and students who wish to explore the Septuagint's historical and linguistic context.

Another significant modern translation is the Septuagint by Alfred Rahlfs, revised by Robert Hanhart. Known as the Rahlfs-Hanhart Septuagint, this translation adheres more closely to formal equivalence, providing a critical text that is faithful to the Greek manuscripts. It is widely used in academic settings and serves as a foundational text for Septuagint studies. The Rahlfs-Hanhart edition includes a critical apparatus that documents textual variants, making it an essential resource for textual criticism and scholarly analysis. This translation's emphasis on accuracy and fidelity to the original text makes it a valuable tool for in-depth study and research.

The Orthodox Study Bible (OSB) is another important modern translation that incorporates the Septuagint. The OSB is unique in that it combines the Septuagint with the New King James Version (NKJV) of the New Testament, providing an integrated biblical text used by the Eastern Orthodox Church. This translation adopts a formal equivalence approach while also considering the liturgical and theological traditions of the Orthodox Church. The OSB includes extensive commentary, theological notes, and liturgical references, making it a comprehensive resource for Orthodox Christians and those interested in Eastern Christian theology.

The Brenton Septuagint, translated by Sir Lancelot C.L. Brenton in the 19th century, remains a significant reference for English-speaking readers. Although it reflects older translational practices, the Brenton Septuagint has been widely used for its accessibility and fidelity to the Greek text. It adopts a more literal approach, making it a valuable resource for those seeking a traditional rendering of the Septuagint. Despite its age, the Brenton Septuagint continues to be used in academic and religious contexts, providing a historical perspective on Septuagint translation.

Another noteworthy translation is the Lexham English Septuagint (LES), which aims to provide a modern and accessible rendering of the Septuagint while maintaining a high degree of fidelity to the original text. The LES employs a balanced translational philosophy, striving to preserve the meaning and nuance of the Greek while presenting it in clear and contemporary English. This translation includes extensive footnotes and cross-references, aiding readers in understanding the textual and historical context of the Septuagint. The LES is particularly useful for those who wish to explore the Septuagint in a format that is both scholarly and readable.

The New Septuagint Translation (NST) is another recent effort to render the Septuagint into modern English. The NST adopts a dynamic equivalence approach, focusing on making the text accessible and engaging for contemporary readers. This translation emphasizes readability and aims to convey the theological and literary qualities of the Septuagint. The NST includes introductions and explanatory notes that provide context and background information, helping readers to understand the significance of the Septuagint in the broader biblical tradition.

The influence of the Septuagint on contemporary translations extends beyond its own textual tradition. Many modern translations of the Old Testament, such as the NRSV and the Revised English Bible (REB), incorporate insights from the Septuagint when translating the Hebrew Bible. These translations often reference the Septuagint in their footnotes and critical apparatus, highlighting significant differences and alternative readings. This practice enriches the translation process by providing a broader perspective on the biblical text and its interpretative history.

The translational philosophies and approaches to the Septuagint vary widely among modern translations, each offering unique insights and contributions to biblical scholarship. Formal equivalence prioritizes fidelity to the original text, while dynamic equivalence emphasizes readability and accessibility. Notable modern translations of the Septuagint, such as the NETS, Rahlfs-Hanhart, OSB, Brenton, LES, and NST, reflect these diverse translational philosophies and serve different purposes for scholars, students, and religious communities. The Septuagint's influence on contemporary Bible translations underscores its enduring significance in the study and interpretation of the Scriptures, providing a rich and multifaceted resource for understanding the biblical text in its historical and theological context.

Chapter 10

Theological Reflections on the Septuagint and New Testament

Christological Interpretations

The Septuagint holds a crucial place in Christian theological tradition, particularly in its Christological interpretations as illuminated by New Testament writings. These interpretations underscore the theological and doctrinal continuity between the Old and New Testaments, with the Septuagint often serving as a foundational text for understanding and articulating the nature and mission of Jesus Christ.

One of the most significant aspects of Christological interpretation in the Septuagint is its use in the fulfillment of Old Testament prophecies concerning the Messiah. The Gospel writers frequently cite the Septuagint to demonstrate that Jesus is the fulfillment of these prophecies. For example, in Matthew 1:23, the evangelist quotes Isaiah 7:14 from the Septuagint, which renders the Hebrew word "almah" as "parthenos," meaning "virgin." This translation underpins the Christian doctrine of the virgin birth, affirming that Jesus' birth was a fulfillment of the prophetic sign given by Isaiah. The Septuagint's wording here plays a pivotal role in shaping the Christological understanding of Jesus' nativity.

The Psalms, as rendered in the Septuagint, also carry significant Christological interpretations. Psalm 22 (21 in the Septuagint), famously quoted by Jesus on the cross with the words, "My God, my God, why have you forsaken me?" (Matthew 27:46), is seen as a prophetic foreshadowing of the Messiah's suffering and crucifixion. The vivid descriptions of suffering and deliverance in this psalm are interpreted by New Testament writers and early Christian theologians as typological references to Jesus' passion. This psalm, along with others like Psalm 110:1 ("The Lord said to my Lord, 'Sit at my right hand, until I make your enemies your footstool'"), underscores the messianic kingship and divine authority of Jesus, as acknowledged in the New Testament (Acts 2:34-35).

Isaiah 53, often referred to as the Suffering Servant passage, is another critical text in the Septuagint that receives a Christological interpretation. The detailed portrayal of a servant who suffers and dies for the sins of others, described in the Septuagint with striking terms such as "he was wounded for our transgressions, he was bruised for our iniquities" (Isaiah 53:5), is applied to Jesus' atoning death on the cross. This passage profoundly influences Christian theology, particularly in understanding Jesus' role as the sacrificial lamb who takes away the sins of the world (John 1:29).

The Septuagint's translation of various titles and names also carries Christological significance. For instance, the term "Christos" (Χριστός), meaning "Anointed One," used in the Septuagint to translate the Hebrew "Mashiach" (Messiah), becomes central in the New Testament as a title for Jesus. This title appears extensively in the Gospels and the Epistles, affirming Jesus as the anointed Messiah promised in the Old Testament. The use of "Christos" in the Septuagint thus lays the groundwork for its pervasive theological use in early Christian writings.

The book of Daniel in the Septuagint includes notable Christological elements. Daniel 7:13-14 describes the vision of "one like a son of man" coming with the clouds of heaven, a figure who is given dominion and glory and a kingdom. Jesus frequently refers to Himself as the "Son of Man," notably in passages like Mark 14:62, directly linking His identity and mission to this messianic figure described in Daniel. The Septuagint's rendering of this vision emphasizes the divine authority and eschatological role of the Son of Man, which is integral to Christological thought.

In the book of Wisdom, part of the Deuterocanonical books included in the Septuagint, there are significant passages that Christian tradition has interpreted Christologically. For example, Wisdom 2:12-20 describes the persecution of a righteous man who claims to be the Son of God. Early Christians saw this as a prefiguration of Jesus' own suffering and rejection.

This text, while not part of the Hebrew canon, holds an essential place in the Septuagint and provides additional depth to the understanding of Jesus' life and mission.

The Gospel of John particularly illustrates how the Septuagint shapes Christological interpretations. John 1:1-14 presents Jesus as the Logos, the divine Word through whom all things were made. This concept of the Logos has parallels in Hellenistic Jewish thought, influenced by the Septuagint's translation and interpretation of Old Testament wisdom literature. The identification of Jesus as the Logos integrates Jewish and Hellenistic elements, portraying Him as the pre-existent divine agent of creation and revelation. This integration underscores the theological depth of the prologue of John's Gospel, linking it to the broader biblical narrative found in the Septuagint.

Furthermore, the book of Hebrews extensively uses the Septuagint to argue for the superiority of Jesus' priesthood and sacrifice. Hebrews 1:6-8 quotes Psalm 45:6-7 and Deuteronomy 32:43 from the Septuagint, interpreting these texts as referring to Jesus' divine sonship and kingship. Hebrews 8:8-12 also quotes the Septuagint version of Jeremiah 31:31-34, emphasizing the establishment of a new covenant through Jesus. The use of the Septuagint in Hebrews demonstrates how early Christian writers employed this Greek translation to articulate and substantiate their theological claims about Jesus.

The book of Acts also reflects Christological interpretations based on the Septuagint. Peter's sermon in Acts 2:16-21 quotes Joel 2:28-32 from the Septuagint, proclaiming the outpouring of the Holy Spirit as the fulfillment of Joel's prophecy and linking it to Jesus' resurrection and exaltation. Similarly, Acts 8:32-35 recounts Philip's encounter with the Ethiopian eunuch, who is reading Isaiah 53 from the Septuagint. Philip explains how this passage refers to Jesus, leading to the eunuch's conversion and baptism. These examples illustrate how the early Christian community relied on the Septuagint to interpret and proclaim the significance of Jesus' life, death, and resurrection.

The theological concept of the "New Covenant" is deeply rooted in the Septuagint's translation and interpretation. The phrase "New Covenant" (καινὴ διαθήκη) in Jeremiah 31:31-34 is prominently quoted in the New Testament (Luke 22:20; 1 Corinthians 11:25; Hebrews 8:8-13), highlighting the fulfillment of God's promise through Jesus. The Septuagint's rendering of this passage emphasizes the transformative and enduring nature of the new covenant, which is foundational to Christian theology and the understanding of Jesus' redemptive work.

The Septuagint also contributes to the understanding of Jesus' role as the "Good Shepherd," a theme prevalent in the New Testament. In Ezekiel 34, the Septuagint describes God's promise to shepherd His people and to set up one shepherd, "my servant David," over them.

Jesus' self-identification as the Good Shepherd in John 10:11-18 resonates with this imagery, portraying Him as the fulfillment of God's promise to care for and guide His flock. The Septuagint's depiction of the shepherd motif enriches the Christological interpretation of Jesus' pastoral and sacrificial role.

The use of the Septuagint in patristic writings further illustrates its Christological significance. Early Church Fathers such as Justin Martyr, Irenaeus, and Origen frequently cited the Septuagint to support their theological arguments and to demonstrate the continuity between the Old and New Testaments. Justin Martyr, in his "Dialogue with Trypho," argues that the Septuagint foretold the coming of Jesus as the Messiah, using it to engage with Jewish interlocutors and to affirm the legitimacy of Christian claims. Origen's Hexapla, a critical edition of the Hebrew Bible with parallel Greek translations, underscores the importance of the Septuagint in early Christian scholarship and exegesis.

The Christological interpretations of the Septuagint in light of New Testament writings reveal a profound theological continuity and depth. The Septuagint serves as a vital link between the Hebrew Scriptures and the New Testament, providing the linguistic and conceptual framework for understanding Jesus as the fulfillment of Old Testament prophecies and promises. Its influence extends to the titles, themes, and motifs used to describe Jesus' identity and mission, shaping the Christological thought of the early Church and enriching the theological discourse of subsequent generations. The Septuagint's role in this interpretative process highlights its enduring significance in Christian theology and its contribution to the comprehensive understanding of the biblical narrative.

Old Testament Prophecies and Fulfillment

The fulfillment of Old Testament prophecies in the New Testament, particularly through the lens of the Septuagint, is a cornerstone of Christian theology, highlighting the continuity and divine orchestration of the biblical narrative. The Septuagint, as the Greek translation of the Hebrew Scriptures, was the version most frequently used by early Christians and the authors of the New Testament. This translation not only facilitated the spread of Christianity in the Hellenistic world but also profoundly influenced the interpretation and understanding of prophetic fulfillment in the life and mission of Jesus Christ.

The Septuagint's rendering of Isaiah 7:14 is pivotal in understanding the prophecy of the virgin birth. The Hebrew text uses the word "almah," which generally means a young woman of marriageable age. The Septuagint, however, translates this word as "parthenos," explicitly meaning "virgin." This translation is cited in Matthew 1:23 to support the claim that Jesus' birth to the Virgin Mary was a fulfillment of Isaiah's prophecy. This interpretative choice underscores the theological assertion that Jesus' birth was a divine intervention, setting the stage for His messianic role and affirming His divine origin.

Another significant prophecy is found in Micah 5:2, which foretells that the Messiah would be born in Bethlehem. The Septuagint's translation of this passage aligns closely with the Hebrew text, and this prophecy is directly cited in Matthew 2:6 when the Magi seek the birthplace of Jesus. The precision of this geographical detail enhances the claim that Jesus' birth was in accordance with prophetic scripture, emphasizing the fulfillment of God's promise through specific historical events.

The Septuagint's translation of Zechariah 9:9, which describes the coming of a humble king riding on a donkey, is quoted in the New Testament to depict Jesus' triumphal entry into Jerusalem (Matthew 21:5, John 12:15). This scene is central to the Christian understanding of Jesus as the peaceful and humble Messiah, contrasting with the expectation of a militant deliverer. The Septuagint's phrasing captures the humility and meekness of the prophesied king, reinforcing Jesus' identity as the servant-king who fulfills God's salvific plan.

Psalm 22, a poignant depiction of suffering and deliverance, is frequently associated with Jesus' crucifixion. The Septuagint's translation of this psalm includes vivid descriptions that resonate with the New

Testament accounts of Jesus' passion. Phrases such as "they pierced my hands and my feet" (Psalm 22:16) and "they divide my garments among them, and for my clothing they cast lots" (Psalm 22:18) are seen as direct foreshadowings of the events surrounding Jesus' death. These parallels are drawn in the Gospels (Matthew 27:35, John 19:24), highlighting the fulfillment of scriptural prophecy through Jesus' suffering.

The Suffering Servant passage in Isaiah 53 is another profound example of prophetic fulfillment. The Septuagint's translation emphasizes the vicarious suffering and atonement of the servant, with phrases like "he was wounded for our transgressions, he was bruised for our iniquities" (Isaiah 53:5). The New Testament writers, particularly in the Gospel of John and the epistles of Paul and Peter, interpret Jesus' crucifixion as the ultimate realization of this prophecy. This connection underscores the theological concept of Jesus as the sacrificial lamb who takes upon Himself the sins of humanity, providing redemption and reconciliation with God.

The book of Daniel, specifically the vision of the "Son of Man" in Daniel 7:13-14, is crucial for understanding Jesus' self-identification and messianic mission. The Septuagint's depiction of the Son of Man coming with the clouds of heaven and receiving an everlasting dominion is echoed in Jesus' words during His trial before the high priest (Matthew 26:64, Mark 14:62). This imagery not only affirms Jesus' divine authority but also connects His mission to the eschatological hope of the kingdom of God, as prophesied in Daniel.

Reflecting on the ongoing theological relevance of the Septuagint for modern Christian thought, it is clear that this ancient translation continues to inform and enrich contemporary biblical interpretation and theology. The Septuagint bridges the Old and New Testaments, providing a textual and interpretative link that enhances the understanding of prophetic fulfillment in Jesus Christ. Its influence extends beyond the early Christian period, shaping doctrinal developments, liturgical practices, and exegetical traditions throughout Christian history.

In contemporary theology, the Septuagint offers valuable insights into the interpretative practices of the early Church. Understanding how early Christians read and applied the Septuagint helps modern scholars and theologians appreciate the historical and cultural context of the New Testament. This awareness fosters a deeper engagement with the biblical text, encouraging a holistic approach that considers both the Hebrew and Greek traditions.

The Septuagint also plays a critical role in ecumenical dialogue, particularly between Eastern Orthodox, Roman Catholic, and Protestant traditions. Each of these traditions recognizes the Septuagint's significance in different ways, and engaging with this shared heritage can promote mutual understanding and respect. The

Septuagint's textual variations and unique readings offer a broader perspective on the biblical canon, enriching theological discourse and fostering a more inclusive approach to scriptural interpretation.

The Septuagint's influence on modern Bible translations underscores its enduring relevance. Many contemporary translations, such as the New Revised Standard Version (NRSV) and the New International Version (NIV), reference the Septuagint in their footnotes and textual apparatus, highlighting significant differences and alternative readings. This practice enhances the accuracy and depth of modern translations, providing readers with a fuller picture of the biblical text's transmission and interpretation.

In liturgical contexts, the Septuagint continues to shape the worship practices of many Christian traditions. The Psalms, as rendered in the Septuagint, are integral to the prayer and hymnody of the Orthodox Church, and the Septuagint's readings are often used in lectionaries and liturgical readings. This continuity of use underscores the Septuagint's role in the spiritual life of the Church, providing a scriptural foundation for worship and devotion.

Theologically, the Septuagint's Christological interpretations remain a fertile ground for reflection and exploration. Its translations and renderings open up rich avenues for understanding the person and work of Jesus Christ, inviting contemporary theologians to delve deeper into the connections between the Old and New Testaments. The Septuagint's portrayal of messianic prophecies, sacrificial themes, and eschatological hope continues to inspire and inform theological discourse, offering a profound resource for articulating and deepening the Christian faith.

The fulfillment of Old Testament prophecies in the New Testament, as seen through the Septuagint, highlights the divine orchestration and continuity of the biblical narrative. The Septuagint's translations and renderings play a crucial role in shaping the Christological interpretations of the New Testament writers, emphasizing the fulfillment of God's promises through Jesus Christ. The ongoing theological relevance of the Septuagint for modern Christian thought is evident in its influence on biblical scholarship, ecumenical dialogue, liturgical practices, and theological reflection. This ancient translation continues to serve as a vital link between the Hebrew Scriptures and the New Testament, enriching the understanding and interpretation of the biblical text for contemporary Christians.

Conclusion

Studying the Septuagint and Greek New Testament together is of enduring relevance, offering profound insights into the early Christian understanding of Scripture. The Septuagint, as the Greek translation of the Hebrew Bible, provided the scriptural foundation for the New Testament writers and the early Church. This translation served as the primary Scriptures for Greek-speaking Jews and early Christians, shaping their theological concepts and interpretations.

The Septuagint's influence on the New Testament is evident in the numerous quotations and allusions found within the Christian canon. By examining these texts together, scholars and believers can better appreciate the continuity and fulfillment of Old Testament prophecies in the New Testament. The Septuagint's translations of key passages, such as Isaiah 7:14 and Psalm 22, often emphasize messianic themes and foreshadowings of Christ, providing a rich tapestry of prophetic fulfillment that underscores the divine orchestration of salvation history.

The linguistic and stylistic features of the Septuagint and the Greek New Testament reveal a dynamic interplay that enhances our understanding of both texts. The Septuagint's use of Hellenistic Greek, with its distinct idioms and structures, influenced the language of the New Testament writers. This linguistic connection facilitates a deeper comprehension of theological concepts and narrative techniques employed by the early Christian authors.

Moreover, studying these texts together allows for a more nuanced interpretation of key theological themes such as covenant, redemption, and eschatological hope. The Septuagint's translation choices and interpretative nuances often illuminate the theological intentions of the New Testament writers, providing a richer context for understanding their messages. This comparative study enhances the depth and breadth of biblical exegesis, fostering a more comprehensive and integrated approach to Scripture.

The Septuagint also played a crucial role in the theological development of the early Church. Church Fathers such as Origen, Augustine, and Jerome engaged extensively with the Septuagint in their writings and exegesis. Their reliance on this translation reflects its authority and significance within early Christian thought. By studying the Septuagint alongside the Greek New Testament, we gain insight into the interpretative methods and theological reflections of these early theologians, enriching our own understanding of Christian doctrine and practice.

Furthermore, the Septuagint's influence extends to contemporary biblical translations and scholarship. Modern translations often reference the Septuagint to clarify ambiguous passages, resolve textual variations, and provide alternative readings. This practice highlights the ongoing relevance of the Septuagint as a critical resource for biblical interpretation and translation. Its contributions to textual criticism and manuscript studies continue to inform and refine our understanding of the biblical text, ensuring its accuracy and fidelity for future generations.

In addition to its scholarly significance, the Septuagint's influence on Christian liturgy and worship is profound. Its readings were integral to early Christian liturgical practices, shaping the spiritual formation and theological understanding of believers. This liturgical use underscores the Septuagint's role as a bridge between the Jewish and Christian faiths, fostering a sense of continuity and shared heritage.

The impact of the Septuagint on biblical studies and Christian theology is multifaceted and far-reaching. Its translation of the Hebrew Scriptures into Greek opened the door for the spread of Jewish and Christian teachings throughout the Hellenistic world, laying the groundwork for the global dissemination of the Christian faith. The Septuagint's interpretative nuances and theological emphases have shaped the development of Christian doctrine, influencing key debates and controversies throughout Church history.

Final thoughts on the impact of the Septuagint underscore its vital role in the formation of the Christian canon and the development of biblical scholarship. The

Septuagint's translations provided a framework for the early Church to articulate and defend its beliefs, contributing to the formation of creeds and doctrinal statements that continue to define Christian orthodoxy. Its textual variations and manuscript traditions have enriched the field of textual criticism, offering a window into the historical transmission and preservation of Scripture.

The ongoing study of the Septuagint and Greek New Testament together fosters a deeper appreciation for the interconnectedness of the biblical narrative and the theological continuity between the Testaments. This integrated approach enhances our understanding of God's redemptive plan, as revealed through the Scriptures, and informs our faith and practice as contemporary believers. The Septuagint, as a bridge between the Hebrew Scriptures and the New Testament, remains a cornerstone for theological inquiry, spiritual formation, and the pursuit of a deeper, more nuanced faith. Its enduring relevance and impact on biblical studies and Christian theology testify to the richness and complexity of the biblical text, inviting us to engage with Scripture in a thoughtful, informed, and reverent manner.

Made in the USA
Columbia, SC
24 January 2025